A Volunteer Nurse on the Western Front

About the Author

Olive Dent was an elementary school teacher, who volunteered as a nurse in World War I, and served in a tented hospital in Northern France for two years. As well as writing this memoir, originally published as *A V.A.D. in France*, she also contributed regularly to the *Daily Mail* and *The Lady*. She died in 1930, aged 45, in the care of a Marie Curie cancer hospital in London, where there was a ward named after her.

A Volunteer Nurse on the Western Front

OLIVE DENT

With illustrations by
R. M. Savage and others

2 4 6 8 10 9 7 5 3 1

First published in 1917 by Grant Richards Ltd, London

This edition published in 2014 by Virgin Books,
an imprint of Ebury Publishing

A Random House Group Company

Every reasonable effort has been made to contact copyright
holders of material reproduced in this book. If any have
inadvertently been overlooked, the publishers would be glad to
hear from them and make good in future editions any errors
or omissions brought to their attention.

940.47541

www.randomhouse.co.uk

Addresses for companies within The Random House Group Limited
can be found at: www.randomhouse.co.uk/offices.htm

The Random House Group Limited Reg. No. 954009

A CIP catalogue record for this book is
available from the British Library

The Random House Group Limited supports the Forest Stewardship
Council® (FSC®), the leading international forest-certification
organisation. Our books carrying the FSC label are printed on FSC®-
certified paper. FSC is the only forest-certification scheme supported
by the leading environmental organisations, including Greenpeace.
Our paper procurement policy can be found at:
www.randomhouse.co.uk/environment

Printed and bound in England by CPI Group (UK) Ltd, Croydon, CR0 4YY

ISBN: 978075355774

To buy books by your favourite authors and register for offers, visit:
www.randomhouse.co.uk

My thanks are due to the Editors of the Daily Mail, *the* Evening News, *the* Yorkshire Evening Post *and* The Lady *for permission to use some matter – a small part only – which has appeared in their pages.*

WINTER QUARTERS: THE TEMPORARY HOME OF A MEDICAL OFFICER

CONTENTS

Illustrations

Chapter I

A Kitchener Nurse

'What have I done for you,
England, my England?
What is there I would not do,
England, my own?'

WAR! ENGLAND AT war! It couldn't be. It must be some frightful mistake. War was the prerogative, the privilege, the amusement of the vague, restless, little kingdoms, of the small, quarrelsome, European States and far-distant, half-breed peoples. War was an unreality not to be brought to *our* land, not to be in any way associated with England, with *our* country.

And yet – and yet – there was the dreadful, numbing, awful news in the paper, and newspapers would not dare publish anything untrue which was

1

prejudicial to the common weal. People with serious expression and tortured thoughts tried to cope with the gravity, the enormity, the surprise of the situation. The dim, almost nebulous fear of years had actually materialised. England was at war! Fire, slaughter, dripping bayonet, shrieking shell, – how were they going to affect us? What was to be done?

One looked at one's dear ones at home with a passion of over-mastering love. One caught one's self looking at strangers in the street, on the bus, and in the railway train, – at that worn little mother with the tired, trouble-haunted eyes, the laughing girl-child with the soft, rounded limbs, the crooning baby with his whole, wondrous future before him. Who was to defend them all? For the first time in a happy, even life one felt bitterly resentful of one's sex. Defence was the only consideration in the popular mind in those early August days. And defence was a man's job, and I, unfortunately, was a woman.

Some one quoted Kingsley to be fiercely contradicted. True enough, the women would weep, and weep in full measure, but that was no reason for an apathetic acceptation. Meantime there was surely work to be done.

But what work?

Some few of us registered the names of, and arranged visits to, the families of soldiers and sailors immediately called up for service, and the sight of those pitiful, pathetic, utterly helpless families made our hearts ache and strengthened our determination to be up and doing. There came a call for men and more men. The regulars and the reservists had marched away to the war. Motley bands of recruits in ill-assorted mufti fell into line and nobly ambled off to be made into soldiers.

No call had yet come for nurses. And yet the New Army of men would need a New Army of nurses. Why not go and learn to be a nurse while the Kitchener men were learning to be soldiers?

The nursing profession was at that time regarded as very inhospitable to outsiders. No doubt we should be despised and abused, considered as very raw recruits and given only the donkey-work to do. Well, it would not be done any the less efficiently, through having studied as much as possible the science and art of nursing. Besides, weren't the regulars, from mildly despising the Kitchener men, veering round to a well-merited appreciation and trust? That might happen in nursing. At any rate, auxiliary nursing service would assuredly be required. I would be a Kitchener nurse.

Like every other woman at the time I reviewed my own particular case and weighed up matters. I had had a two-years' course of hygiene and physiology in college, a half-yearly session at advanced physiology later, had done St. John's Ambulance work for two or three years, and, provided I had a good aim in view, am what schoolboys term a good swotter. Not a great deal to go on, perhaps. Still it was a beginning.

I resurrected my nursing books, bought others, re-attended St. John's Ambulance lectures and practices, and was fortunate in joining a detachment whose members used to visit hospitals on observation tours, and also used to enter civil hospitals for service, during as many hours of the day as could be arranged.

If, at the time, I should have needed any spur to my enthusiasm, if I had needed any strengthening of my determination to nurse, I should have received such fillip in plenty. For Belgian refugees soon came to us, piteous little bands of people made apathetic by an exhausting succession of stupendous sorrows and fled from pillaged houses with all their world's goods held in a string bag or a bundled sheet. They told us of those terrible days on the packed jetty at Ostend where men died and babies were born and people went mad. Frail old ladies, such as Rembrandt immortalised, were there, old men rich in years and poor in physical strength, young girls with terror-laden eyes, a blind boy. Think of it, – of the horror of hearing the first dreadful news of the oncoming of Uhlans, of the interminable stumbling along the white, sun-baked roads, of physical sufferings, of anxieties untellable, of a confused journey to a strange country where even the sounds were unfamiliar, – all in the maddening, inexorable darkness.

And then our own fighting men came back from the war, *our* boys with shattered limbs, gaping flesh wounds, bruised, battered bodies.

> '*Ever the faith endures,*
>   *England, my England:*
> *Take and break us: we are yours,*
>   *England, my own.*'

England had taken and broken them, and still there were so very many of us women doing nothing of value, nothing that counted. Events were proving that it was abroad where nurses were more urgently required. The war zones of the Western Front and Gallipoli were busy. Personal inactivity was galling. I had no ties. I could give my whole time to nursing, so disliked the thought of auxiliary, part-time work in England. I volunteered for foreign service, was accepted, inoculated, vaccinated and asked, in August 1915, to undertake service in Egypt. For private reasons I was compelled regretfully to refuse, but enthusiastically accepted service in France in the late summer of 1915.

Chapter II
En Avant

MONDAY. SPENT THE morning at St. John's Ambulance Headquarters where we were provided with arm brassards, identity discs, and identity certificates in place of passports, the latter most unflattering documents containing a terse, crude and unvarnished account of our personal appearance, age and address. The morning was bitterly raw and cold, but not even the order to prepare for life under canvas damped or chilled our ardour. Spent the afternoon at the stores in a chaos of other V.A.D.s, pukka nurses, khaki men and confused assistants. Bought a camp bed, camp chair, camp bath and camp basin, – they all look refractory and sullen, – a ground sheet, a sleeping-bag, gum-boots, an oil-stove and a collapsible lantern.

Tuesday. Our party of a hundred V.A.D.s – members of St. John's Ambulance Association, St. John's Ambulance Brigade and the British Red Cross Society – left Charing Cross Station this morning. It may be the station of Infinite Sorrows, of heart-breaking farewells, but our going, at any rate, was quite unheroic.

The place was very crowded with nurses, khaki men and officers, and a sprinkling of business passengers, and there may have been tears and piteous partings, but most of us were too busy attending to hand luggage, camp kits, vouchers and corner seats to be either observant or to listen for anything in the minor key.

We had a very good and very quick crossing with not even a floating bottle to deceive ourselves that an enemy submarine was near. Only warships, dull grey from funnel to watermark, cruised around, and our escort hugged us close. I had been thrilled a few days before in reading the account of a well-known journalist who described himself sitting on deck in his life-saving jacket. He must have had a bad attack of 'cold feet,' for in our case such a precaution was not taken by any one, not even by one of our most popular princes who happened to be aboard.

Arrived at Boulogne, the passengers 'travelling

Military' were straightway disembarked, and we nurses went to an hotel where we were allocated to various hospitals, – all in Northern France, – and to which we were to proceed on the morrow. It was here we saw a new aspect of hotel life. I shared a room with a girl I had never before seen. It was seven feet by nine, with a sloping roof having two rafters and a skylight, and with lime-washed walls. Ce n'est pas magnifique mais c'est la guerre. War accommodation, and the bill next morning was a war bill!

As we went downstairs a small crowd of other V.A.D.s were standing round a bedroom door shrieking with laughter. They invited us to come along to 'their room' and then we laughed too. The room looked like a picture after Hogarth. It contained five beds, three of them fat, French, wooden beds, two of them little iron ones, and it had lately been vacated, or rather was about to be vacated, by some officers. The bedclothes were lying about in piled heaps, there was a kilt, a Sam Browne, a couple of revolvers, a tin of tobacco, some cigarettes, haversacks and spurs and, tied to one of the bed posts, . . . a huge hound. He stood with drooping ears and tail, looking so very sheepishly and apologetically at us that we all laughed helplessly. Some one controlled herself sufficiently to pat him, and he whacked a great tail strenuously from side to side looking more ludicrous than ever...An Active-service bedroom, evidently.

We had tea at a café beloved of peacetime days. The room was crowded with khaki, – the cakes as good as ever and the proprietor and staff casual as ever at presenting *l'addition* and taking pay. We waited so long for our *addition*, that we thought we might be charged ground-rent, and we amused ourselves with the French poodle who begs for oblong pieces of sugar to be placed on his nose – sugar was plentiful then! – at the 'brass hats' foraging for *éclairs* and *petits fours* with the pertinacity and perseverence peculiar to a brass hat, and at the variety in mackintoshes and trench-coats – some with a *flair,* some *en Princesse,* some belted, some collared in lambskin, some high to the ears like a wimple and so on. As we returned to the hotel, we shop-gazed, and became enamoured of a delectable blouse in ivory crepe-de-chine with tiny, lapis lazuli buttons. Then we scolded ourselves, – for this was only our second day in uniform, – and whipped the offending Eve out of us.

Wednesday. We walked along to the Casino passing on our way the garage where were drawn up in a line upwards of a hundred ambulance cars of all makes and many of them gifts, e.g., from the British Farmers, from the County of Berkshire, from the Salvation Army, and so on. It was a very good sight to see so many fine cars smartly drawn up with their bonnets in line as though some one had called out briskly, and in stentorian tones, ''Shun. By the left, DRESS.'

On by tram to Wimereux. Passed a company of British 'bantams' marching along singing to the accompaniment of a mouth organ, and with a rag-tag and bob-tail following of bare-legged Boulounnaise fisher-girls and old men, zinc buckets on arm. We wondered idly what the British Tommies first thought of things, – of the Boulounnaise women with woollen pants to ankles, and bare feet slipped into heelless sabots, of the mistress of the *charcuterie* who dusts the sausages displayed in the shop window with a feather duster, of the little boys called in by *maman* from play and deprived of their black, sateen pinafore to be arrayed in outdoor costume of goat skin coat, Homburg hat, buttoned boots and socks, – and of what the French first thought of the British Tommies especially, say, on occasion when in throaty unison they announced:

'O – o – ah, it's 'snice ter get up i' th' moarnin',
But it's snicer ter lie in bed;'

11

or when in mournful accents they declared:

'*Old Soldiers never die, never die, never die,*
Old Soldiers never die,
They fade away.'

Without doubt it must be difficult for the French and certainly an occasional strain on their *entente cordiale* feelings and intent to have their towns, their trams, their cafés, their restaurants, their streets and shops overrun with us British as is the case in Boulogne, Havre, Rouen, Abbeville, Amiens and most of the towns of Northern France. We English would assuredly have found it so if French people had been garrisoned at York and Leeds, Birmingham and Leicester. One wonders if we would have been as for-bearing, as gracious, as friendly as our neighbours are under the circumstances.

At Wimereux we climbed up to the cemetery, which has been extended to include a military section for the fallen British. Long lines of smoothed graves, each headed with a little wooden cross, – it is a picture of majestic simplicity, of infinite pathos, nothing tawdry, nothing trivial, nothing but the grandeur of simplic-ity. We think of the poor, maimed bodies, all that remain of that grace of English youth and comeliness, of the beauty that is consumed away, of man turned to destruction. We think of Time who unheedingly dims the proud stories of those valiant heroes. Each little, smoothed grave means a tragedy, a gap in some home across those dark waters. Our age has paid its price for the nation and the race. Those are the dead who won our freedom. May we cheat Time, and ever retain the thought. May it compel us to greater patience, greater fortitude, greater forbearance in the work that is to come.

We turn from the graves and leave our dead to their bravely-earned rest on the little wind-swept hill. May they sleep in peace.

Chapter III
A Chilly Reception

WE LEFT THE Gare Maritime shortly after 2 p.m. The train loitered leisurely onwards for the next twelve hours. Some V.A.D.s went to Etaples where the big S.J.A.B. hospital is situated, some went to Havre, some to Le Treport, some to Versailles to the Palace Hospital there, some to Rouen.

The journey was interesting enough while daylight lasted. We waved to all the British Tommies we passed, and they cheered and waved energetically in return, and we interrupted two games of Soccer by throwing from the carriage window illustrated papers and cigarettes.

At Noyella two French Red Cross nurses came with collecting boxes and, later, distributed bread and coffee to the troops. One, who happened to be dressed in indoor costume, white from head to foot, looked very dainty and charming as she stood smiling good-bye, and to her a disappointed Tommy called in mock angry tones, 'Arrah, begone wi' ye, ye little baste. Niver a drap nor a crumb hae ye geen mi. Wait till ye come to ould Oireland,' the which she evidently regarded as some gracious speech for she beamed on him and smiled anew.

Here, too, two French officers descending from our compartment flicked out a golosh belonging to one of our girls. The sight of a brilliant, blue-clad, gold-braided, medal-emblazoned figure bowing and presenting a characteristically English, size-six golosh on the palm of his hand was deliriously funny.

At the end of our railway journey we learnt that the hospital to which two of us were allocated was a tent hospital situated on a racecourse three or four miles out of the town. We climbed into a waiting ambulance car, the mackintosh flap at the back was dropped, and we shot off into Stygian darkness – cheery! Once we heard 'Croix Rouge m'sieu,' and saw a flash of a lantern – evidently some 'barrier.' Then the car pulled up, and we tumbled out to be received by the night superintendent nurse. Still more cheery!

We were taken to the night duty room, and in about

three minutes' time were wondering why on earth we were so consummately foolish as to volunteer for nursing service. It was 2.30 in the morning, the door of the duty room was swollen and would not close, an icy draught played along the floor, the kettle refused to boil for some time, though finally some very weak tea was made. We were most impolitely hungry, for we had not been able to buy food on the railway journey, and we could cheerfully have eaten twice the number of meagre-potted-meat-plentiful-bread sandwiches provided. The sister lucidly and emphatically explained to us that she had no idea what 'people were thinking about' to send out such girls as we, girls who had not come from any 'training school,' girls who had 'not had any hospital training,' – what use could we possibly be?

We had before heard unheeded tales of the edged tongues of women of the nursing profession, tales to which we refused to give credence. That early morning hungry, cold, tired, with little fight in us, and no inclination to dilate on our own various qualifications, we came within an ace of believing them. Fortunately, however, neither of us were either overwhelmed with, or impressed by, our manifold shortcomings. Also we were so lacking in awe as to prefer having more faith in the knowledge of the Government than the opinion (or possibly the prejudice) of an individual nurse. To the credit, too, of the said nurse and her profession let me record that, in less than a month's time she was a staunch friend, and between us all there was mutual liking and respect.

Our meal ended, we were taken to a wooden hut which we learned afterwards had just been finished that day, – carpenter's tools, trestles and shavings were lying round. In each of our bunks was a camp bed, a soap box on which stood a wash-bowl and a candle, – all lent us because our kit had not got through. We sternly shut out all thoughts of our home bedroom and bed, and hurried into the camp apology.

Thursday. On duty in the wards.

CHAPTER IV
Camp Nursing

THE FIRST DAY'S duty in a camp hospital is a perplexing, nonplussing affair. Primarily, I wasn't certain where I was. For a bird's eye view of the camp would have revealed a forest of marquees and a webbing of tent-ropes. The marquees sometimes clustered so close that the ropes of two roofs on the adjoining side were not pegged to the ground, but were tied overhead, the one to the other, so supporting each other and saving space. Between such dual marquees was a tarpaulin passage, usually spoken of as a tunnel.

Each row of marquees was known as a 'line,' and named as a letter in the alphabet. Thus 'A' line consisted of eight or nine tents, known as A1, A2, A3, and so on. All these marquees were exactly alike, and as we nurses passed from one to the other several times in the morning, it was at first a little difficult to know whether one was in A1, A3, or A5.

Later, one grew to recognise each by certain little signs and symbols, this one because the floor squeaked, that one because a small hole was burnt in the side, that one because it had a little rent near the door, that one because it had had an extra dose of colouring material, used to render the marquees less noticeable and also waterproof, and that one because it was nearest the sisters' duty bell-tent.

The early morning's work consisted of making twenty beds, dusting twenty-four lockers, taking twenty-four temperatures, and tidying the wards. Then came a snack lunch, and a change of apron followed by the giving of the necessary medicines, a couple of inhalations, the applying of two or three fomentations, a small eusol dressing, the dispensing of one or two doses of castor oil, and the cleaning of a linen cupboard.

Then came the boys' dinner for which most of the up-patients went to the (marquee) dining-hall, leaving only two boys sitting at the ward table. They ate their meal with the keenest Tommy Atkins enjoyment, heads low over the business, knife and fork plying energetically over stewed rabbit and baked potatoes.

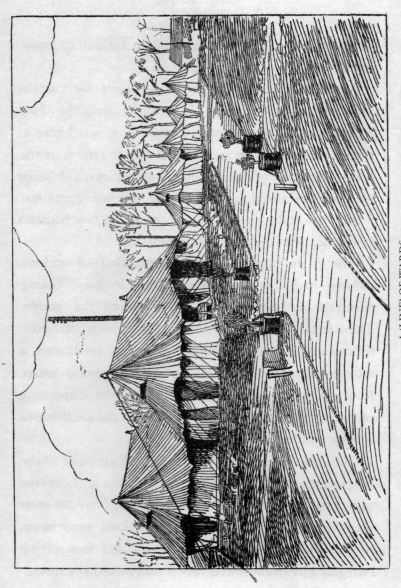

A 'LINE' OF WARDS

Watching them was a bed-patient with acute gas-tritis and on 'no diet.' Silence, but for the hardworked cutlery and then in the very driest of Cockney accents came the bed-patient's remark: 'Ite, drink and be merry, fer ter-merrer yer snuffs it.'

In the afternoon, more medicines were to be given, the washing of patients was to be done and the beds made. At five o'clock came tea and off-duty.

The newcomer to a camp hospital finds matters very different to what she has been accustomed in England; no hot water, no taps, no sinks, no fires, no gas-stoves, a regular Hood's 'November' of negation. She probably finds the syringe has no suction, that all the cradles are in use, and there is none for the boy with bad trench feet, that there are only six wash-bowls for the washing of a hundred and forty patients, and that there is nothing but a testing stand, and a small syringe with which to help the medical officer through a dozen typhoid inoculations.

These drawbacks seem a little depressing and over-whelming at first, but the adaptable girl soon learns to overcome such minor difficulties. None of them are insurmountable, and if she conspires with sorry Fate she can soon mould things nearer to her heart's desire.

Thus, the absence of taps, hot water, and sinks one chafes against for two or three days, and then gets accustomed to the existing conditions and substitutes. The syringe will have better suction if the piston be wrapped round with a few strands of white cotton from one of the boys' hussifs. Two boards tied together with strings in a V shape can keep up the bedclothes as effectually as a cradle, while the needle of the inoculation syringe can be sterilised by holding it with a pair of forceps in a test tube of boiling water.

On active service it is a case of improvising, improvising, improvising, and one article in its time plays many parts. Thus the other day a hut door was being propped open with a tin of bully beef – the beef being subsequently eaten at the night orderlies' supper. Once, too, we had an enamelled pie-dish, a curious thing for us to possess; no one knew how we came to have it. That pie-dish was used for the sterilisation of instruments, wash bowl, filled with moss as a receptacle for forest flowers, for fomentations, once for the making of a linseed poultice and as a *bain-marie*. The only thing I never saw it used for, was the baking of a pie.

Its uses, by the way, I haven't given in chronological order!

The casual reader may wonder that there should be

much improvisation and some people may affirm that the correct equipment ought always to be there. Such a statement, however, would be an utterly thoughtless one. The correct equipment is not always either imperative or essential. And with an army, only the essential in the way of equipment counts. Brains and forethought, – or otherwise, common sense, – must substitute immense amounts of baggage.

Incidentally, the curtailing of baggage explains much of the 'pinching' and borrowing that goes on in the Army, a practice to which every one sooner or later descends, – no, I mean resorts. The private property of an individual is sacred, the Government property is only held on a very insecure lease.

Thus if one wants paraldehyde in E lines, and F lines has some, then obtain it. If A lines has a syringe, and your need is too desperate to await getting it through a proper channel, secure G's syringe. If you want paraffin for the heating of a patient's feed and D has more than they require, beg, borrow or steal D's surplus, but get it. Of course, playing the game as one does, the paraldehyde goes back immediately, the syringe is sterilised and returned, you render to Caesar the paraffin that is Caesar's directly you get your daily issue. Failing this, you are 'a rotter' and the whole camp soon knows the fact and safeguards itself against you.

'Pinching' is always quite an accepted condition of affairs. Meeting an orderly carrying some planks of wood on his shoulders the other morning, I said in somewhat slipshod fashion, 'And what are you making yourself, Smith?' 'As usual, sister, I'm making myself a thief,' came the unhesitating reply. All the consolation the late owner of any article may receive is the overworked tag, 'You're unlucky, mate. You shouldn't have joined.'

Active-service nursing, like all other nursing, is intensely fascinating and interesting. The men come practically straight from the trenches, and are deeply grateful for, and appreciative of, the cosy beds, the nicely-cooked food, the absence of vermin, the cleanliness and brightness of the wards, and our attempt to make them comfortable and happy. They have not grown irritable with the tediousness of long nursing or wearisome convalescence, and they have the excitement of a forthcoming trip to 'Blighty' to cheer them.

On the nursing side one has the pleasure and satisfaction of quick results and rapid progress. A jaw case, say, comes in with some of the flesh shot away by high explosive, the surrounding skin spotted with small black patches, clotted and caked with blood, dust and clay in the moustache.

One syringes and washes the wound with peroxide followed by a lotion, shaves the face where necessary, washes the skin with hydrogen peroxide, or ether soap and warm water, continues to syringe the wound frequently and dress it with eusol, until, at the end of a few days, – three or four, perhaps, for jaw cases are notoriously quick in healing owing to the good circulation of blood in the face, – the patient is ready for evacuation to England.

It has been a pleasure and delight to have the wound progress so quickly, and the work has been thoroughly enjoyable, but now comes the little disappointment of active-service nursing. One does not see the completion of the case, the subsequent grafting and building which ultimately makes so wonderful a cure for the poor boy.

Active-service nursing is distinctly chequered, here to-day and there to-morrow, wherever the work is heaviest, and with unexpected happenings occurring with nonplussing frequency. The time-table person who doesn't like to be disturbed from the even tenor of her ways would find little joy in it. By which I have no intention of conveying the suggestion that routine and methodical work are at a discount. They were never more essential. In addition, extra demands are made on one's resource, one's adaptability, one's originality, one's power of organisation, one's ability to cope with a great, and often unexpected, influx of work, and one's faculty for seizing on the essential and omitting the trivial, – quite probably a matter of vital importance.

Chapter V
'Convoy In'

Iᴛ ɪꜱ ɴɪɴᴇ o'clock in the morning, the ward work is completed and the dressings about to begin. In each dual marquee the floors and lockers have been scrubbed with cresolis and water, the beds have been made, the linen chest, food cupboard and dressing-box – courtesy titles, by the way, they are only packing cases, – which stand in the tunnel between the marquees have been cleaned and put in order, the table scrubbed and set out with lotions, drums and dressing materials, and one puts on one's gown preparatory to taking down the dressings while looking forward to a good, uninterrupted morning's work.

> *'Lints, splints, bandages and cod-liver oil.*
> *Fall in A, fall in B,*

Fall in all the company.
Fall in at the double.
Fall in at the double.'

So sounds the bugle, and the stretcher-bearers hurry off. The interruption has already come. A convoy is in.

In the course of a few minutes the tent-door parts and our cases arrive, usually as many as we have empty beds. The walking cases are in khaki, clay covered, mud-stained, blood-stained, clothing ripped, head perhaps bandaged, arm in a sling or hand bandaged, face boasting pads of gauze and adhesive plaster or, perhaps, foot in huge 'trench slippers,' – in which latter case the patient is probably carried in pick-a-back.

Each patient has his temperature taken and is, if necessary, fed. The walking cases are given a seat by the stove pending an inquiry into the nature of their injuries, and one goes to see the stretcher cases installed ready to have their blanket bath. The older patients meantime look on very interestedly, adding jest and jibe to the welcome extended.

'Now, laddie, what is the matter?'

'Oh, they caught me in the back, sister.'

'Serve him right for running away, doesn't it, sister?' says the stretcher-bearer, as he very gently helps him on to the bed. A smile from the damaged gladiator shows that he takes the 'chipping' in the right spirit.

'And you, old chappie?'

'Not too bad,' is the revealing reply.

'Ah! You're an Australian.'

'Sure, sister,' giving me an answering smile. 'Dinkum.'

A case with a leg in box-splints waits a minute until we push under the biscuits (a mattress is in three pieces each known as a 'biscuit') a fracture board.

'Somebody been pulling yer leg, mate?' asks his neighbour.

'No, just got my pad on. I'm batting next innings.'

'What's the damage here?' one asks while glancing at the field card of a boy who, it seems, has inflammation of the cellular tissue of the feet, – briefly indicated as I.C.T.,' – and as one passes on, one overhears his little joke related to his neighbours. 'The M.O. at the field dressing station looked at my feet, prodded them, pinched them, poked his fingers at them, and didn't know what to say so finally he wrote down I.C.T. – I can't tell.'

Meantime the newest arrival is claiming attention – a young boy with bad trench feet, purple, red, swollen, and with big black blisters from which later

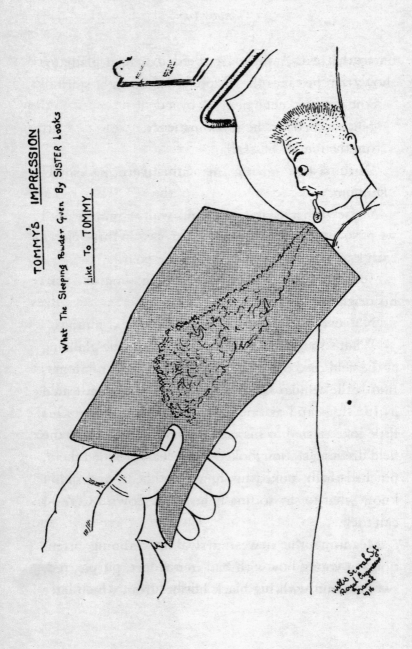

TOMMY'S IMPRESSION

What The Sleeping Powder Given By Sister Looks

Like To TOMMY.

we get a great amount of fluid. As he is being very carefully transferred from stretcher to bed, one talks in the manner made familiar by a dentist, and with the objective of distracting the patient's attention a little from the matter in hand.

'I think you're the baby of this ward, sonny.' The stretcher is raised on the level of the bed. 'How old are you? Sixteen?'

'No, sister, nineteen.' I take each foot while an orderly lifts him bodily.

'Nineteen! Oh, surely not so old. Sixteen, and you're a drummer boy,' slipping a cushion under his calves and arranging a 'cradle.'

'No, sister.'

'What! Are you really a soldier with a rifle to fight with!' I am tucking in the bedclothes. He gives a sly little smile and a drop to his voice.

'No, sister. The Army doesn't give yer a rifle ter fight with. It gives yer a rifle ter *clean*.'

I dutifully laugh and go to another tent in the line, – a 'line' consists of four, six, eight or nine marquees according to the division, surgical or medical, and according to the cases, heavy or light.

In this tent the newcomers have already been put to bed, and look up expectantly to see what kind of reception is accorded them. Occasionally boys have subsequently confessed to me they didn't like at all the thought of coming to hospital. They 'had an idea the sisters were strict,' – a politely vague term which presumably covered all the supposed feminine short-comings which ever existed.

'Good-morning, boys – two, three – five, six new guests at our hotel.'

'Yes, sister,' says the orderly. 'And we charge seven and sixpence a day for bed and breakfast, don't we?'

'Certainly, and other meals at *à la carte* prices. Nursing and medical attendance a guinea a day. Hope no one has lost his pay-book.'

A general smile at the little nonsense, and every Tommy Atkins of them is at ease.

The walking cases usually go to the steam-bath and how they do enjoy the visit, especially when it happens to be weeks since they had their last bath! The bed-patients are blanket-bathed. Meantime khaki and trench clothing have been hurried out of the ward with all dispatch, since the fight against vermin is most strenuous, most vigilant, and ever unceasing.

The dressings taken down, the wounds are seen by the medical officer and the dressings done. A meal follows, a cigarette, and then the boys go to sleep. And how they do sleep – deep, heavy, stupefying sleep it is! Poor, weary, buffeted humanity! Thank Heaven for an infinitely precious boon.

Only one wakeful boy among the newcomers, and he assures me he doesn't feel like sleep, the bed is too soft. Oh yes, he is quite comfy; it is cushy, *très bon,* he is affirming, *cinq bon.* I overhear the latter, a new piece of slang to me, and immediately my footsteps are stayed.

'And why *cinq bon*?'

'Five *bon*, sister.'

'Yes, but why five?'

'Oh, five *bon*, sister, a nap hand.'

I have spoken of the occasional aversion which some of the boys confess to have wholly needlessly harboured against hospital life. Another feeling, natural enough, I suppose, but equally needless and ungrounded is that of fear. Many of our patients are sturdy young Britons who have never had any ache or pain more dangerous or severe than toothache in all their healthy young lives, and to them 'hospital' is a word which expresses a world of woe, which ought really to be writ all in capitals. They imagine surgeons with large, long knives and hawk-like eyes ruthlessly walking up and down ready to 'chop.' They imagine severe sisters, fully armed with terribly efficient forceps, ready to pull determinedly at all caked dressings and bandages. They have in their youth heard eloquent parents give exceedingly intimate, and exceedingly inaccurate, accounts of the troubles that befell them in such and such hospital 'when I had a crool time of it, me dear,' and when 'I lay on me back five months on end.' They have, too, at more recent date reverentially listened to the accounts of healed warriors, – personal and embellished accounts of hideous sufferings, accounts picturesquely told in billets at night when conversation otherwise might have languished.

No wonder a little fear of hospitals is engendered within them.

It is our privilege, pleasure and pride to dispel that fear, – a pride which actually grows to a conceit. It is very feminine to enjoy rising above expectations, and to hear stumbling expressions of gratitude after a dressing, – to be assured that 'it feels luvly' or 'I was dreading that, sister, and it didn't hurt a bit' – is as the sound of music in one's ears. It is a form of vanity of which we are not ashamed, indeed, we revel in it. We try as hard to gain such compliments as any actress ever works to 'get over' the footlights, as hard as any

passé professional beauty fishes for her toasts of yester-
year. We treasure those whispered thanks more dearly
than ever we treasured whispered conservatory compliments, for we know the one is sincere, whereas. . . .

Most nervous patients are reassured by 'chipping,'
for 'chipping' is the language they best understand. It
is so much more human and cheery than the 'minister-
ing angel stunt.'

'Now, little chappie, swinging the lead, eh? We'll
soon fix this up. Nothing very much the matter, is
there?' and with a soak of hydrogen peroxide and
warm sterile water, caked dressings soon give way.
The clay-covered, blood-spattered surrounding skin is
washed with the same lotion or with ether soap and,
possibly, an area shaved – as in the case of head and calf
wounds – and the wound itself is cleaned and dressed.

'Is the plugging out, sister?' a boy will sometimes
ask, when one takes up the bandage to bind up the
wound – and then, of course, one does feel conceited!

'Is it a Blighty one, sister?' we are invariably asked,
perhaps by the owner of a gaping gash three or four
inches long.

'That scratch a Blighty one! Good gracious, boy,
you'll be marked "Active" very soon. Still, of course,'
altering the tone of voice, 'in three or four days' time

the medical officer is sure to have too many Blighty tickets to carry round, and we might persuade him to get rid of two when he reaches your cot.'

Such a beatific smile dawns that there is nothing to be seen above the bed-clothes but two crescents of inflated cheek and a wide, red mouth. And he is left to his beatitude.

Unfortunately, there are times when our little nonsense talk of welcome is stilled, when we hurry round – or send an orderly – to see that each case is comfortable, while we give our whole attention to one in particular. For he has come in with the ominous, red-bordered field-card and the syllable 'Sev.' following the diagnosis, e.g. 'G.S.W. rt. humerus sev. cpd. frac. rt. femur,' indicating a gunshot wound of a severe character and a compound fracture. Possibly the journey to hospital has aggravated the poor boy's injuries, the jolting of car or carriage may have brought on a haemorrhage or has exhausted strength already much enfeebled.

More blankets and hot water bottles, the saline bag and the hypodermic needle play their part or, perhaps, after the consultation comes an immediate visit to the theatre, or perhaps... 'All you can do, sister, is to make him comfortable. A third of a grain of morphia...'

Then follow some of the bitterest moments one is called upon to endure, – to feel an intensity of helpless pity, to chafe against a surging feeling of impotence, to watch, to wait and yet to do nothing, nothing of any telling value. One welcomes any little need of the patient's. One poor boy one night whispered, 'I don't know what I want. I seem to be slipping away,' and at his request there were changed and changed again the pillows, the cushions, the position of the limb, the cradle, the bedclothes, his lips were moistened, his face wiped and then he spoke again.

'I know now why you nurses are called "sisters." You *are* sisters to us boys.' With a lump in the throat, and stinging tears at the back of the eyes one could only silently hope to be ever worthy of the name.

Chapter VI

Active Service in the Snow

SNOW HAS FALLEN persistently for a fortnight. Its coming was presaged by leaden skies and dull grey shadow clouds, which delighted the Australian and New Zealand nurses who were unaccustomed to half-lights, and some of whom had never seen snow. Then one morning we awoke to find the camp mantled in whiteness, the tents roofed and the tent ropes powdered with fairy-poised flakes, while a flaming, early sun shot red shafts of light through a silhouetted fringe of tall poplars, whose high branches dangled clumps of mistletoe like so many deserted rooks' nests.

The New Zealanders especially were charmed, but, *nous autres*, we all shivered into our warmest woollies, packed them tight on us like the leaves of a head of lettuce. 'Positively I shall have to peel myself tonight,' vowed one girl. And, indeed, it takes a good many woollen garments to replace the furs and fur coats to which we have accustomed ourselves within the past few years. Finally, one gets into one's clothes, laces up one's service boots – how long they are! – with clumsy chilblained fingers, or thrusts and stamps one's feet into gumboots, having first donned two pairs of stockings, one pair of woolly 'slip-ons,' or a pair of fleecy soles, and probably padded cotton, or cyanide, wool round the toes. Then with a jersey, a mackintosh, and a sou'wester over one's uniform, out into the snow to the messroom, with no path yet made. It is one of the few times one pauses to remember that one is 'on active service.'

Of course, almost every one has a cold, almost every one has a cough, and every one has chilblains. Some unfortunate creatures have all three. Our chilblains, true to their inconvenient and inconsiderate kind, have cracked, and the disinfectants among which we dabble in the wards, while keeping them aseptic, give them never a chance to heal.

So each day, like Henry V's veterans, we count our wounds and scars and say – well, we say many things.

Cures? We dutifully rub on, and in, liniments while lacking faith in their efficacy. One brave soul the other night, driven to drastic measure by continuous irritation, walked boldly out into the snow in her bare feet. Some critics deplored her foolhardiness, some deplored her grandmotherly superstition and quackery, while we others stood round the door and applauded the courage of her action, though shivering at the sight of its stoic execution. Unfortunately for the complete success of the cure, she trod on a sharp stone.

In the wards the patients are mildly excited over the snow, as being a new diversion. 'Sister, may I take you tobogganning this afternoon?' asks one boy with a bandaged head and a broken femur, but otherwise very cheerful. 'Thanks so much. I should love it, and Jock will take me skiing, won't you?' I retort, whereat Jock laughs, for he is but very slowly 'coming round' again after 'making a meal of a few bits of shrapnel,' as he terms his poor abdominal injuries. 'And you others – well, I think we might manage a bob-sleigh party, eh?' 'Oh, rather, sister!' says a boy, peering over the top of his bed-cradle, which, by the way, he will need for many long weeks.

Round the tent door stand the up-patients, eager to seize any chance surreptitiously to snowball orderlies and the French newspaper boy, and then to take mean advantage by an instantaneous retreat into the 'dug-out.' We hurry on with the morning work and its attendant duties and dressings, and as the afternoon and evening come, so, too, does the snow, faster than it can be raked from the tent roof and path. The stoves are filled with coal and coke, the tents are laced closely, blankets are hung purdah-wise over the lacings, the gramophone is kept busy, cards, draughts, and puzzles are brought out, and everything is '*très bon*, sister,' as the boys say, 'quite merry and bright.' Only occasionally the minor tone is introduced: 'There's a few boys in the trenches would like to be here to-night.'

The snow has ceased to fall when we leave at eight o'clock to go to the quarters, and the whiteness of the snow gives considerable light, We meet the night nurses coming on duty dressed *cap-à-pie* in wool and mackintosh, and looking like so many Lucy Grays coming with their lanterns through the snow. Lacking the decorum of Lucy, they shy some painfully well-placed snowballs at us, so we dip for a handful of snow. 'Oh! hit me, but don't hit my "hurricane"!' sounds like a mean advantage, so we, stony-heartedly, cry, 'Put your "hurricane" at the leeward side of you – Fore!' At other times it has been blowing a blizzard when we have exchanged duties, and then all we call is a 'Good-night,' with occasionally the soldier cry, 'Sorry you joined, draftie?'

Going to bed is a prodigious rite and ceremony. After a bath in a camp bath, which against the feeble force of chilblained fingers has a maximum resistance, immovability and inertia, and yet seems to possess a centre of gravity more elusive than mercury, one dons pyjamas, cholera belt, pneumonia jacket, bed socks, and bed stockings as long and woolly as a Father Christmas's, and then piles on the bed travelling rug, dressing gown, and fur coat. Even in bed the trials of active service do not end on occasion. We found one girl lying in bed the other night with her umbrella up. The snow had melted and was trickling through the tent, and she was too tired to trouble about having matters righted, 'I'm imagining it is a garden parasol, and I'm in a hammock, and it's June.' Gorgeous imagination!

But this morning the rain has come, and we are as glad as the Ancient Mariner to see that rain, for to us it means the passing of the snow. Our camp has looked charmingly picturesque with the surrounding hills receding to a dim blue haze, a Futurist sun arrogant at dawn and sunset, and honey-gold at noon, sentinel trees, tall and gaunt, long, straight roads peopled occasionally by dark lines of passing soldiers, their marching muffled by the snow, their singing dying away as they quickly reach that distance where they look so much like toy soldiers. Poor boys! For their sakes more than our own we are glad to welcome the rain. Picturesque the snow may be, but the practical side of it is cruel.

Chapter VII

From My Diary

A GLORIOUS AUTUMN afternoon. Went for a walk through the forest and met a big draft on its way up the line. A magnificent body of men, clear-eyed, bronze-faced, swinging tread. Their style of marching gave a good indication of their excellent fitness, for they simply swept along even although they were all wearing 'tin-hats' and were weighed with the full 'humpy.' Worming her way in and out between the troops was an old crone selling apples.

What a pity we nurses have no kind of salute! I should dearly love to show the 'boys going-up' some little respect, just as I always want to pay tribute when I pass a soldier's funeral. Walking on I stopped at a tree and began to pick ivy for the wards from its trunk. Another draft went past and one rogue began to sing, and soon every one else joined in:

> *'Just like the ivy, I'll be constant and true,*
> *Just like the ivy, I'll cling to you.'*

I am becoming a complete nurse. I dab on the backs of my heels when I walk. I swish my skirts. I can lend an air of festivity to a ward with a clean towel, two red ties and a few green leaves. I know there are as many clean ends to a sheet as Euclid had sides to a square. I make beds with all the overturned sheets dressing from the left (or right), and with corners as exact as though a protractor had been at work, and as smooth as though a spirit level had been requisitioned. It seems a pity to lose the art, so I incline to being a chamber-maid after the war. Or perhaps a post of bedder at Cambridge might prove more lucrative. A bedder is a woman with a black bonnet, no conscience, and an acquisitive instinct. I must secure the one, get rid of the other, and develop the third.

I have just had a most enjoyable meal. That sounds a very greedy remark, but when I add that the meal was breakfast in bed, on active service, it will be interpreted as the acme of luxury, self-gratification and self-indulgence. Breakfast in bed, is, of course, only possible when one is ill – and I am brutally healthy – or when one has a 'day off,' and the latter is of a Spartan infrequency; my last was nine weeks ago.

The home-sisters are supposed to bring the breakfast to us, but they are always so busy that a kindly-disposed friend saves them the trouble by bringing it along on her way to the wards. W— and B— brought mine this morning, each wearing that smile of reflected *glee*, – indeed, I might describe it as a grin, – which is ordinarily dispensed to the lucky possessor of a 'day off.'

'What a gorgeous breakfast,' I cooed. 'I only need the morning papers and my letters, for it to be absolutely a breakfast *de luxe*.' The gorgeous breakfast? Well, it was on a japanned tray, which has seen very active service, and lost much of its veneer in the battles. It was guiltless of a traycloth and, of course, there was no serviette. However, a uniform cap soon supplies that deficiency.

The teapot lid had its knob knocked off these many days ago. *Pas de quoi*. The tea was piping hot and delicious. The marmalade was enthroned in an egg-cup, Army pattern, blue enamel, bringing to one's

A SUNNY DAY

mind somehow the tea-shop term 'one portion.' The sugar-basin was an emptied potted-meat jar. 'Dis-used' jar I had nearly written, but it is anything but that, – its uses are legion. The milk jug's origin was ditto. The plates were as far beyond reproach as Caesar's much-vaunted wife, and were filled with a rasher of admirably cooked ration bacon, and crisp toast made from the excellent Army bread. A pat of delicious butter from a neighbouring French farm completed the total. Truly a gorgeous breakfast! I felt a sybarite.

A girl comes to an adjacent bunk. 'U-u-u-gh! Where are my gum boots and sou'wester? It is snowing again. I knew it was going to do something offensive by the colour of the sky. Of course, I'm on the offensive about the occurrence, but—'

'Napoo, napoo,' shout several voices. I chuckle, then snuggle down.

Took a dozen of the boys to church this morning, – a beautiful little service. The church is a marquee and the bell is rung by striking a suspended, empty shell-case with a piece of old iron. The tent floor has been stained brown with solignum, and we have a few forms to sit on. Our chancel is marked off by two primitive rails and backed by four brown screens, the reredos being of cream cloth stretched tightly, the top fringed with a little gold fringe. The service is beautifully simple, the hymns those well-known ones we have all sung since we were children, the 'sermon' a few minutes' topical address on, say, 'The Trenches of Life,' 'The S.O.S. Call,' 'The Making of an Attack.' Then 'Let us pray for victory, for those at home whom our absence has made desolate, for the navy and those in responsibility, for the sick and especially those in our hospital, for the triumph of the right, for the coming of peace.' We all stand up at attention after the final hymn and sing the National Anthem, our feminine voices quite drowned by the men's, and then, with the boy-blues, we all troop out into the soft, spring sunshine.

Across the road is a large hall, one given by the Boy Scouts of Britain, and to it come any troops resting in the neighbourhood, for a day or two, on their way up the line. When the hall is packed with a khaki congregation of a thousand or more, it is a wonderfully impressive sight, especially when the heads are reverently bowed in prayer.

In the evening our boys may go to an adjacent Y.M.C.A. hut, where a lantern service is held. I went last Sunday evening. The hymn 'For those in peril on the sea' was thrown on the screen. At the piano was a patient with a crutch at either side of him, poor boy. He played and we all sang lustily. Then came a prayer for help in our work and our life, and courage to meet death in its season. We had the hymn 'Jesu, lover of my soul'; some scenes, accompanied by verbal comments, of life in the Holy Land, and lastly, the hymn 'Oh God our help in ages past.' It gave one an overpowering feeling of sadness to stand there in the darkness, singing:

> *'Time, like an ever-rolling stream,*
> *Bears all its sons away;*
> *They fly forgotten, as a dream*
> *Dies at the opening day.'*

Our generation ended, these brave boys individually will be forgotten, but their deeds, dream-like in their amazing valour, have opened up a new day of freedom and independence which can never be forgotten. What a gift to posterity!

We had a mail in to-night, the first for five days. One girl on her way to dinner called at the office on some errand, discovered the letters sorted, and took upon herself the glad task of playing postman. Accordingly, she appeared in the mess carrying a great bundle of correspondence in her apron.

Dinner was almost ended, and there was a general stampede towards a deserted table. We would have made a good picture for an illustrated paper as we all crowded round, a huddled mass of grey, white and red, heads and caps bobbing, aprons fluttering, hands greedily outstretched, the impatient mounted on chairs, the artful below burrowing their way determinedly to the front like so many sappers, the decorous, – or perhaps the merely inept, – contenting themselves with the outer fringe.

A delayed mail is nearly as exciting as a Christmas mail. We are all greedy and insatiable, no matter how many letters we get. Newspapers we neglect and ignore, ingrates that we are, even going so far as to say 'Only newspapers, how disappointing!' though knowing well we will resort to them for home gossip with gusto on the morrow.

'I don't like *embarras des richesses* even in the matter of a mail,' says a cautious Scotch soul next door. 'I like to spread out my joys as I do my possessions, and make them go far.'

But, seated among the débris of five letters and two

parcels, I, like a bacchante, laugh her to scorn. I love my joy in extravagant draughts.

Since the 'Sister Dora' cap is taboo, and we have the handkerchief cap with which to tie up our head, one V.A.D. has cut her hair short in the fashion of the bob-crop of American children. She quite rightly argues long hair to be an unnecessary waste of time and energy, – unnecessary since her head must never now be uncovered except in her own bunk. One called her a wise Virgin, but we others contented ourselves by dubbing her a strong-minded female, the while conservatively and foolishly retaining our own questionable crowning-glories.

Goaded to action by absent friends, two of us – V.A.D.s – went to be photographed this afternoon. We mounted interminable stairs eventually to find the occupants of the studio eating rissoles round a gas stove. We selected our scenery with the idea of eliminating the florid, while the operator selected our attitude and posture with the idea of including the picturesque, clamped irons behind us and stood critically before us. 'Si triste, trop triste,' we were abjured. 'Pas belle, pas belle,' we were assured – a truly nasty blow. 'Un petit plus gai. L'air joyeux,' we were invited. 'Comme ça, comme ça,' we were exhorted as he licked his lips north, south, east and west. We obeyed in a comparative degree while he twisted our heads to a revue-girl, picture-postcard allure. This we disobeyed in very positive degree, remembering Devonshire House, and finally giving us up as a bad bargain he shrugged his shoulders until they were almost on a level with his parietal bones, hopelessly squeezed the bulb, and extravagantly bowed us out past his cardboard Watteau terraces, and his *papier-maché* eighteenth century pedestals in superlative disgust. We left in subdued mood, conscious of our shortcomings in the matter of English stiffness.

A drizzling November afternoon so B— and I borrowed an umbrella before going for a walk in the forest. The owner of the umbrella having recognised that our nursing staff, like the Apostles, have most things in common had taken the very necessary precaution to fasten on the handle a luggage label bearing her name!

Up a very steep and rugged pathway an old, old crone was tugging a handcart piled high with faggots. So B— and I pushed behind. Turning her head at the unexpected lightening of the load, – for she evidently thought some of the faggots had fallen, or the cart like the chords of Tara's harp had come asunder, – she showed us a face so ludicrous in its dismay and amazement as to make a delightful study. Our lack of conventional decorum astounds and mystifies the French.

Like silly children we walked on and on not thinking of our return journey so were very glad to accept the lift afforded us by some English Tommies on a steam-roller. Even more astounded looks from the French passers-by!

A dreadful day. The morning bitterly cold, and the fires refusing to light. The boys put on paraffin and soon the marquees were full of fumes. Then the wood smoked until it seemed as though we would all be kippered. Five convoy patients warned for England. They and their wounds to be dressed in forty-five minutes. A convoy in. Several patients to X-ray and some for operation; two of latter rather bad and very busily sick. No off-duty, but took quarter of an hour to go to the dentist to have a tooth stopped. A hectic evening, dressings, beds, diet-sheets, blighty tickets, temperatures, etc., etc. Frost very severe and only half a pailful of water obtainable. Caught my finger on a bed-rail, overturned and broke the nail. Very tired and cold. No fires in the mess, and only half a jugful of water for washing and hot bottle. The wick of my oil stove dropped into the well. My chilblains particularly energetic. I had indigestion and no *aqua menth pip* and a tactless neighbour persisted in singing 'When you come to the end of a perfect day.'

The country now is lovely, great hanging sheaves of wistaria, laburnum and lilac, the chestnut spires reared in pink and white profusion, and in the meadows round the camp hosts of buttercups, white marguerites, and great yellow daisies.

On the latter I seized with rapture, and then discovered they were plutocratic relations of our John-go-to-bed-at-noon suffering, too, from the very common ailment, swelled head. Only here the ailment justified itself most picturesquely. We have harebells and lovely, blue cornflowers growing wild, and a most delightful, carmine-coloured clover with a conical head which bursts usually into flamingo-pink. The up-patients go out and bring us back armfuls of flowers with which we deck the tents. Lately we have been going to the forest for lilies-of-the-valley, but they are 'over' now, so we have to content ourselves with Geoffrey Plantagenet's flower, the yellow broom. We get great branches of that, – and in our particular wards it appears to best advantage, in a 'vase' which is made out of the case of a British 18-pounder picked up by one of our R.A.M.C. men after Mons.

Camp life in these glorious spring days teems with interest and swarms with ants. Ants! – we have hundreds of thousands of them. 'Maiden aunts, they must be,' says a Scotch patient, 'for they are so fussy and such busybodies.' They invade the annexes, which we use as food cupboards, and though we commend their energy and enterprise, we condemn their violation of the treaties of cleanliness and possession. A tin of jam gets hastily put away over night, then next morning it is a seething black mass. A pot of sugar left for a few hours presents a heaving, black surface the next time one goes to it.

Accordingly we stand all edibles in a tea-bowl, and surround them with a moat of water. The enamelled bread-pan we have on wooden supports which have been soaked in paraffin.

The patients are often quite interested in the wee beasties. Some of them tell us fearsome yarns of the depredations of the white ants in colonies where they have seen service. They call us to watch any particular little cutenesses our own ants display, give adequate admiration to the engineering feats the tiny things occasionally perform, – and only once soundly rated their lack of intelligence, and that was when I found a company in the medicine cupboard. Even then, however, some one vindicated them. 'P'raps they're fed up with the war, sister, and want to go west.'

'May bugs' we have too. One dropped on my bed last night. It was 'Van-in' for he fell on his shiny, russet-red back. He was about two inches long, and I removed him on a newspaper to the front line of trenches as materialised by a ditch in the hedge. Big, fat moths fly in at night and after bobbing round inconsequently for a time invariably flap on one's face.

Bloated, Germanic-looking spiders come up miraculously through the boards in the tent floor, ditto hairy worms with sloshy bodies and busy little iridescent beetles that seem to have much to do, and very little time to do it in. Crickets sit outside our bell-tents and scream piercingly, and in the wet weather there come in snails and rain. To snails we are inured, but before the invasion of the rain we beat a retreat. However, it isn't possible to manoeuvre much a six-foot camp bed in a small bell-tent, and after the drippings of rain have successfully followed the bed in its circuitous movings, there is nothing for the tent's inmate to do but hoist an umbrella, and report the matter in the morning.

But camp-life in fine weather is glorious – glorious are the nights when the nightingale sings in the forest which borders our camp. Glorious are the times when we lie abed looking out on a moon-bathed sky with scurrying mysterious clouds, nights when we tell ourselves that there is no war. Glorious it is to sit and watch a rose sunset fade to mauve twilight, with a honey-coloured moon, – long drawn-out nights when one's life has time to pause, and one takes a moment to think. Then one loses the charm, turns sideways in the deck-chair, swallowing the lump in one's throat, a lump partly occasioned by the beauty of the evening, partly by one's sheer physical tiredness, and partly by the memory of a torn and gaping wound and of a magnificent young life dying behind a red screen in the ward yonder, quickly as the sunset.

Chapter VIII
A B.E.F. Christmas

CHRISTMAS WITH US began a week or ten days before December 25. We weren't afraid of its being long-drawn-out or of palling on the boys, for our hospital is usually just like a glorified casualty clearing-station. Our patients move so quickly. Besides, none of us O.A.S. people are of the blasé or bored type.

Festivities began by some Y.M.C.A. ladies bringing round presents for the patients. These presents were of two well-chosen varieties – useful, and capable of noise – and the men had their choice. The useful kind were notebooks and pencils, and both were soon busily used media for Christmas wishes to Blighty. The others were little sheep, ducks, lambs, etc., which could be made to emit noises travestying a baa, quack, etc. The boys were rather shy, as usual with strange ladies, so I picked up a sheep, made it bleat, declared it awfully fascinating, and generally set the ball going. One of the ladies asked me to accept it as a mascot, and the boys' tongues soon loosened when one of them said it was 'scarcely the thing for sister to be associated with a black sheep.'

The men were very funny about these animals. In one ward they tied Blighty tickets to their coats and filled in the tickets fully – somewhat after this style: 'C sitting. Able to walk on board. No. 19425618, Pte. Spud Tamson. Corps: First Field Canteen, Wet Division. Ship: *Friendship*. Diagnosis: Homesickness Acute. Signed: H. Oppit, Major, R.A.M.C.'

Some 'were willing to sprint on board,' some 'delighted to jump on board'; one diagnosis was 'swinging the lead,' another 'acute wangling,' while a duck had an operation paper tied to it, 'I certify that I am willing to undergo an operation for strangulation, and after the post-mortem to be stuffed.'

Round the hospital are forests from which we got lots of evergreens and mistletoe. Our Christmas trees we garnished with scraps of discarded cotton wool to represent snow, and decorated with crackers, etc. Wonderful results we got from an outlay of a solitary franc. Then the boys cut out mottoes from paper wrappings: 'Christmas Greetings,' 'God bless the lads in the trenches,' 'Heaven bless our sisters,' 'A Happy New Year to all.' The boys had their own way entirely with the decorations, and incidentally pulled one another's legs unmercifully, tied Christmassy ribbons and holly to the big, wooden, extension supports to which one boy's leg was attached, stuck little golly-wogs on top of the cages over injured limbs, tucked mistletoe in the chart-board of a boy with his head and face all bandaged like a mask, warning him 'Now, be careful, sister may want a pair of gloves this Christmas, and you being such a good-looking chap, well, well, well...'

One night the hospital orderlies had, by way of relaxation, a fancy-dress ball. It was held in the Y.M.C.A. hut – what should we out here do without these huts? – and lasted from seven o'clock till ten. We sisters went and looked on at the proceedings after dinner, got on the platform, judged the competition waltzing, and awarded the prize, fifty 'luxury smokes,' for the best costume.

The whole business was great fun. The boys had determined to lend an air of reality to the ball, and almost half had dressed as girls – or should I say as females? – so that when the couples danced together the sight wasn't very incongruous. What did look incongruous was to see every one smoking, the 'flappers' and the 'Duchess of Devon-shires,' the 'pierrettes' and the 'Army sisters,' not to mention the 'matrons.'

Our theatre orderly came as a matron, his get-up being a great success – cap well over the brow, with only two little wisps of fringe showing, trim little black suede shoes and smart stockings, and the usual regulation uniform. He acted the part, too; came and sat with us on the platform, thereby deceiving many of the other orderlies, and was full of jibes. When one of us remarked that he had changed his dress very quickly, for he had been on duty until eight o'clock, he agreed, adding: 'Much quicker than the ordinary matron. But then I'm no ordinary woman.' The great lead-paper star he had on in the place of the usual medal ('The Star, don't you know, much more exclusive than the R.R.C.') came unstuck, so he borrowed a safety-pin from an adjacent V.A.D., saying: 'Thanks, so much, I'll remember you in my next list.'

An Australian unit adjoins ours, so, of course, there were lots of 'Bushmen.' And gee! how they could dance! The two best dancers, to whom we unanimously gave the prize, were Australians. One 'Tassie,' gowned in a kimono lent by a kindly V.A.D., was a fruit-grower, or something of that sort, from Tasmania, evidently much of a dog in civil life, and also no mean cosmopolitan. Certainly he never learnt to boston as he did on a Tasmanian fruit farm. He and his partner bostoned and rag-waltzed until my very toes itched again. They had itched already many days before with chilblains and trench-feet symptoms, but this was a pleasing, irritating, alluring, tantalising itch, that made me long to defy the inviolable Army rule that sisters must not dance on active service.

On Christmas Eve some of the sisters went carol-singing round the wards. I was coming late to the quarters, for I had been 'specialing' a case. It was a perfect night, very mild, raining moonlight, with the valleys great pools of sombre silence, and the air beautifully still, so still that one could hear when a car had its speed changed on a fairly distant hill. The carols sounded inexpressibly sweet, and one sensed, probably for the first time, the holy character of the Christmas festival.

Arrived at the mess I found that some patients who, apparently, had nothing wrong with their lungs, were acting as waits and were singing to those sisters who were at dinner (the latter consisting of busy-time rations of bully beef, potatoes, macaroni cheese, and a cup of coffee).

They made such a pretty Christmas-card sort of picture, – the glass doors of the mess thrown open, the warm light streaming out and catching the dark outlines of sundry tall poplars, the boy-blues grouped round singing, one holding a lighted lantern, the square collapsible sort that has the old-world, 'langthorne' look about it.

Christmas Day we sisters again gave entirely to the boys. We bought them sausages for breakfast, and that, with the hospital's ration of bacon, 'did them proud,' so they said. They had some nice roast beef and the orthodox pudding for dinner, and then we sisters provided their tea. Our boys chose tinned salmon!! (no, thank heaven for our conscience's sake, we are *not* in medical wards), potted meat sandwiches, scones, rice cake, sultana cake, Christmas cake, assorted buns, jellies and fruits, while they received sundry gifts of sweets, chocolates, and nuts through philanthropic channels. This, with crackers and two-penny worth of primrose crinkled paper and a franc's-worth of yellow daisies, made a great show.

Supper was the same menu, for we had provided so as to 'be on the safe side,' but, horrors upon horrors!

what were our agonised feelings on walking into one marquee to find that the men there had saved their dinner bottle of stout until supper, and were consuming it to the foregoing culinary accompaniment! We thought of handing round immediately four grains of calomel or a 'number nine' to every sturdy person present, and then, we considered, a benignant deity looks after people's tummies at Christmas time, so we stilled our many qualms, and next morning no one was a whit the worse.

On Christmas Day the Australian unit near us presented some religious tableaux, a manger scene, the Three Shepherds, the arrival of the Wise Men, and so on. The tableaux were most beautifully staged, especially considering we are on active service, but Australia in play is just as Australia is in work, very thorough, very effective, and, – despite the almost always negative state of conditions, – she always 'gets there.'

Christmas-boxes? Lots of the boys hung up their stockings, and we put in something for each patient in our ward, even if it were only a khaki handkerchief or a piece of fancy soap, with, of course, always a packet or tin of cigarettes. All our bunks for two or three days before Christmas were sights to behold,

– scarcely fighting room for the inhabitant herself, what with bundles of mittens, notebooks, pencils, comforters, scarves, packets of sweets, smokes, etc., etc. Visitors got no farther than the door for the best of reasons. By the way, one patient hung up his – well, as a matter of fact – his pants, and wrote a letter to Santa Claus, asking for Blighty tickets as his Christmas-box, but next morning – 'Narpoo, no bon' – the chimney wasn't wide enough and Santa Claus had presumably passed by. Later on, however, round came the major, felt the man's toes, asked him if his feet felt numb, etc., etc. Then 'C sitting, sister, please' – and the man had got his Christmas-box, and, what is more, was on his way Blighty-wards within two hours.

We ourselves were not so fortunate with Christmas-boxes. For the sake of war economy a Christmas parcel from home was all we allowed ourselves, and great fun we had warming up large plum-puddings over small spirit-stoves, and Blighty mince-pies over biscuit-tin lids held over the aforesaid stoves. Primitive sort of réchauffé, but excellent good they all were, which is typical of the perverse, contrary way cooking has.

Chapter IX

Housekeeping on Active Service

THIS EXTRAORDINARY WAR is in many ways surprisingly ordinary. Men who have dreamed of the panoply of mediaeval war, of the clash and clang of strife, of galloping chargers and uplifted steel find themselves standing in a sodden trench where, for days and days, they never have an opportunity of seeing a German. Or, worse still, they are miles behind the line installing telephones and electric lights. Women who have felt themselves uplifted by the deeds of those pioneers in the Crimean War are called on to housekeep! And yet, of course, electric lights are required, and nursing staffs must be fed, and the practice of putting each man and woman to their trade will in no way mar the efficiency of things.

The nursing quarters of most of the camp hospitals

in France consist of a wooden hut for the mess-and-sitting-room – by the way, it is almost solely the one and very rarely the other, – a shed of some kind for the cook's kitchen, and bell tents, marquees, Alwyn huts, Armstrong huts, and wooden huts for the housing of the staff.

In the early days, some of our nursing sisters had improvised bedrooms from the loose boxes which were near us, in virtue of our being on a race-course. Later, when tents and huts materialised at a quicker rate, these were left for the accommodation of the batmen. Bell tents and marquees were always very popular, being absolutely delightful in summer and very cosy in winter with the aid of stoves. Some nurses who had thoroughly enjoyed life in a marquee during the winter of 1915–1916 were in a rebellious mood at having to go into a hut for some weeks during the winter of 1916–1917.

It was wonderful how pretty and comfortable bunks and bell tents could be made. All the furniture was of the packing-box variety; indeed, once installed, and a few other bunks inspected, we all felt competent to give authoritative advice on how to furnish a bed-boudoir-morning-smoke-drawing-room on a franc and a half. Chest of 'drawers,' whose characteristic was that they did not draw, were built from small boxes on the cumulative principle and by the system of dovetailing. Then a chintz curtain was hung in front. Another chintz curtain served as a wardrobe. Indeed, chintz like charity covered a multitude of sins, the greatest of these being untidiness.

Most ambitious dressing-tables and writing-tables were evolved by standing a sugar-box on end, knocking out the lower side, and nailing on top at the back a small narrow box. These made a brave show stained with permanganate of potash, or, later, when this got rare, with solignum. A camp-bed, too, is easily convertible into a 'Chesterfield,' flanked at either end with one's pillows pushed into pretty cushion-covers. An admirable 'Saxon stool,' too, most of us possessed, fashioned from three sides of a box and stained. In post-war days house furnishers must look to their businesses, for the land will abound with men skilled in the art of dug-out furniture, and maidens nimble at throwing together O.A.S. furniture.

Camp housekeeping was decidedly reminiscent of a picnic. One had the same makeshifts, the same *multum in parvo* with respect to cutlery and dishes, both as regards cooking and serving, the same triumphant adaptation of commonplace articles to

A 'BAIRNSFATHER' BUNK

superior purposes, the same feeling of everything turning out well in the end. Then, too, one had an additional satisfaction, that of being on active service.

Three of us – all V.A.D.s – ran the home and mess, which at the time consisted of between sixty and seventy nurses. We were helped by batmen, all P.B. men, who cleaned the huts and tents, swept and washed floors, attended to our supply of drinking, cooking and washing water, – taps and sinks were unknown luxuries, – mended fires, washed dishes, cleaned and cooked vegetables, cut up and cooked meats, and generally did the heavier work. We planned the menus, laid the tables, carved, served out the different meals, cooked certain dishes, did the shopping, dusted, had the management of the home quarters, e.g. preparing rooms for newcomers, tending indisposed sisters, and were generally responsible for the hundred and one little trifles necessary to the smooth running of affairs.

Man in pursuance of the domestic arts has often been suggested more or less facetiously as a solution of the domestic servant problem. The soldier man in this particular rôle proved himself a curious creature. Some of his virtues he owed to the fact of his being a soldier, and some of his idiosyncrasies to his sex.

Thus his soldierly dispatch and obedience were

most refreshing to any woman subjected to a succession of pert maids who say 'Yes, miss,' and then execute the order at their leisure. Positively at first it was disconcerting to have such instant obedience, to have the batman rise in the midst of washing the floor to go and perform some duty casually mentioned. The Army rule, 'The last order obeyed first,' however, soon sinks into one's mind.

As workmen our batmen constituted the customary problem a man presents, – they always made a big fuss about having the correct tools. Whereas a woman will drive in a nail with a boot, a hair-brush, or a flat-iron, a man must have his tool-bag by him ere he will undertake a little carpentry.

Possessed of this, however, he will work the proverbial wonders. Our mess furniture was a triumph for our men. The sideboard began life as a huge packing-case for medical stores, so did our glass cupboard, our linen chest, our 'wine-cellar,' and our dwarf bookcase, all bravely stained brown and duly polished. Our best plant-stand did much praiseworthy duty, its packing-case pedestal draped in thin green bastiste, and the plant admirably enshrined in a marmite.

Camp housekeeping in France quickly proved itself to be quite an arithmetical affair. Thus if one decided on making scones, immediately there was a little mental arithmetic to be done in ratios and substitutions, with the home quantity as a basis. For example, if half a pound of flour makes sixteen scones, how many are required for sixty people, – with camp appetites, – a quantity which must then be calculated in demi-kilos, those being the weights we had in the kitchen. Then the quantity of butter, sugar, cream of tartar, etc., must be calculated. Similar arithmetical tussles were necessary before making, say, a custard, and sending for the milk, which, by the way, the batman always spoke of as so many 'leekers.'

Over our makeshifts we used to make merry or grow conceited. Biscuit tins were our great refuge for storage, for converting into buckets, and at times for cooking. Coffee tasted delicious from a biscuit tin, especially on a cold morning with several degrees of frost, and at an hour still unusually early.

Bully beef made excellent curry, good shepherd's pie and most appetising rissoles, particularly when served with tomato sauce made active-service style from a tin of tomatoes, heated, sieved, and thickened with a little flour.

Ration biscuits, otherwise irreverently known as dog biscuits, only required considerate treatment to be responsible for quite agreeable puddings and porridge – reminiscent of the schoolroom 'milk' pudding, it is true, but what would you? We are on active service which is the English equivalent of *C'est la guerre*, both of which accompanied by a philosophical smile or a rueful shrug of the shoulders, as the case may be, are supposed to cover a multitude of deficiencies.

Mice, quite an alarming bag of them, we used to catch with a basin, a thimble, and a piece of stick. Our vegetable sieve was a biscuit tin with holes jabbed in with a jack-knife. The sphere of usefulness of things was never confined, too. Our mimosa bloomed daintily as ever from a glass which originally held Florence Cream, while a charmingly bright touch was given by a polished, oblong cocoa-tin holding holly and red berries.

One of the first essentials in camp housekeeping is to rid oneself of all one's tenderly cherished notions, and all one's dearly loved susceptibilities on the subject of housekeeping, so soon as one enters the mess room. We used to disobey every canon of housewifery ritual and emerge unscathed: boil water over a stick fire held together by three bricks, and yet not get the water smoked, have the dishes washed in hot water and soda, and yet the few gilt-edged specimens we possessed obstinately, serenely and successfully retained their gilt for several strenuous months. Our knives we plunged into a jug of hot, soapy water, and yet the handles remained staunchly attached to the blades. The dish washing used to be done at breakneck speed, and although we had upwards of a thousand dishes washed per day, we had no casualties for a fortnight – once, at any rate – so our soldier men set a very good example to the average scullery maid. Indeed, our boys were treasures, though now and again they liked to twit themselves for doing 'women's work.' 'Wouldn't I make a good wife for some one, sister?' one used to ask me, as he slapped a wet flannel round the floor or cut up the bread for meals. Poor boy, he had been very badly gassed in the memorable first Hun attack, and he was still subjected to dreadful, prostrating headaches.

Active-service housekeeping, interesting though it is, soon, however, begins to pall even on the most fervent apostle of the domestic arts.

Housekeeping is an exhaustive business even when one has only a small home family to cater for. How much more is it so when the family is one of sixty-five people and with meals duplicated – breakfast at 7, at 7.30, and then for the night sisters at 8, 'snack' lunch of the buffet variety from 9 to 10, two midday lunches, two teas, two dinners, and invariably some individual meals to keep warm for sisters delayed.

Then, too, much as one wishes to make more comfortable and homelike the life of those hard-working women, yet one cannot have the same vim and enthusiasm, nor experience the same fascination in 'keeping house' for sisters as one does in working for, and tending, our brave boys. So most nurses and sisters gladly shake from their feet the dust of the mess-kitchen and wend their way back to the wards.

Chapter X

The Trials of a Home Sister

SCENE I. *The* HOME SISTER *interviews the* COOK.
Time 9.30 a.m.

HOME SISTER *seated at table in mess. Enter*
CORPORAL.

H. S. Good morning, Corporal.

C. Good morning, Sister.

H. S. What can you give us for meals to-day?

C. [*dryly*]. Well, it's wot have we got.

H. S. I thought you might manage rissoles. That would be a nice change.

C. Yu-u-s. [*Pause, continuing*]. I don't know wot we'll make them of.

H. S. Well, there are the remains of last night's joints.

77

C. Well, there isn't much.

H. S. I'll see what there is. [C. *disappears*.] These men have no initiative – and no interest. What a pity we don't have V.A.D. cooks. Women are so very clever in using up left overs. Just like the French, who can make a really marvellous meal out of a scrap of garlic, a piece of dripping the size of a walnut, and the claws of a deceased pigeon.

[*Re-enter* C. *with dish, whereon extremely clean bones.*]

C. There isn't enough there, yer know, Sister.

H. S. [*in very hopeful voice*]. Oh, I don't know, there are some quite nice pieces there. Besides, you could eke it out with bully. I want you to make two rissoles for each sister. That will be a hundred and thirty [*in a final tone*]. That's settled. Oh, yes, and you might, too, make an extra two dozen for the night sisters.

C. [*aside*]. Well, she has some 'opes.

H. S. Vegetables and milk pudding you'll serve as usual, except that we should prefer them rather better than usual in the actual serving. The potatoes yesterday were very lumpy.

C. Well, that potato-masher you got down town isn't no good, Sister.

H. S. [*interrupting*]. No? I thought myself that a little longer boiling of the potatoes might have improved matters. Now about dinner. Have you any suggestions?

C. [*dryly*]. Well, it's wot have we got.

H. S. I thought of a tapioca soup, – it is so nourishing, – fricassée of chicken, steamed peach pudding with a sweet sauce, and cheese straws, as your share of the meal.

C. [*aside*]. I *don't* think. Her and her fancy ideas. I'll let her see [*turning to* SISTER]. Well, what about the stock, Sister?

H. S. The chicken bones, of course.

C. I'm afraid they're nothing *but* bones, Sister.

H. S. [*in hopeful tones*]. Well, eke it out with bully. [C. *produces bones.*] Good gracious, where are the pieces of chicken for the fricassée?

C. Well, Sister, there are that many dratted dogs about.

H. S. But haven't you got a safe, man?

C. Yes, Sister, only the door hinge has been off this three month.

H. S. I reported the matter. Hasn't it been mended? [*Writes industriously on memorandum.*] To return to the matter of the soup, Corporal.

C. Well, Sister, if you give me a few soup cubes, a tin of tomatoes, a bottle of sauce and a few potatoes to thicken it, I might manage something.

H. S. And in place of the fricassée?

C. Well, Sister, we've got a lot of Maconochie in hand. What if we got rid of some of those? I could put in a couple of penny packets of curry powder and –

H. S. We'll leave it at that. See that the pudding is good.

C. Yes, Sister... pudding. What about the peaches? They hadn't any at the canteen last night, and stores aren't due in till Saturday, and then they'll likely be late.

H. S. [*despairingly, after long pause*]. What do you suggest?

C. Well, Sister, I could give you prunes and custard, but we've had them five times this week. And the apricots'll want soaking, so you couldn't have those very well until to-morrow. And the sisters don't seem to care about raisins. And the bread puddings – oh, well, they're a wash-out. And you'd spotted dick yesterday lunch. And the under-cook, he isn't very handy, so there's no chance of him making you any of these fancy puddings in advance this afternoon. So what do you think about duff and treacle?

H. S. [*icily*]. Suet pudding and treacle, then.

C. And, Sister, I don't see how I'm to manage the cheese straws.

H. S. And why?

C. Well, it's like this, Sister. We're on half-rations and drew no cheese for three days, and I don't suppose I'll get any for another three.

H. S. [*more icily*]. Omit the cheese straws.
[*Pause. Then exit* C.]

H. S. [*soliloquising sighingly*]. It's very, very disappointing somehow, when one tries one's hardest. Let me see, I drew up quite a nice dinner for the sisters to-night, – a tapioca soup, fricassée of chicken with creamed potatoes, steamed peach pudding and sauce, and cheese straws. And what are we to have? – a query soup, disguised Maconochie, suet pudding and treacle...Well, we're on active service. I suppose we must take the rough with the smooth...only sometimes it seems all rough and no smooth.

[*Re-enter* C.]

C. Sister, Jock has been inoculated and will be off duty the next twenty-four hours. My leave has just come through and I've got to go at eleven o'clock. So I don't know how you'll manage for lunch and dinner, with nobody in the cook-house...By the way, Sister, you promised me some cigarettes when I went on leave...

[*Collapse of* SISTER.]

Chapter XI
B.E.F. Nicknames

WHEN A FEW cheery souls, such as the men of
our Army, get together, nicknames inevitably
abound. I have encountered a great many Army-bred
nicknames in the past two years, have been present
at the baptism of some. 'Orderly, I wish you could
find time to give me a shave to-day,' once remarked
a smooth-faced boy of eighteen. 'A what!' came in
chorus from the other more mature men of the ward.
'Orderly, you'll need a microscope or some forcing
lotion. A shave, indeed!' And for the rest of the time
the boy was in the ward, he was known as 'The
Young Shaver.'

It was in the same ward that we had another young
boy who was very fond of chocolate. Hence, although
he was 'a good plucked 'un' and had been wounded

twice he became known to many and sundry as 'The Chocolate Soldier.'

One youngster earned his nickname through mispronunciation. I took his name, number, etc., on admission, and then asked 'What is the trouble, boy?' 'Synoblitus (synovitis) of the right knee, sister.' So Synoblitus he became, which was duly shortened to Blitus, and then got to Blighty – which, poor boy, was more than he got, as the synovitis was too slight to merit an expensive, albeit very pleasant, journey westward.

As among schoolboys, the personal appearance is a fruitful source of nicknames. Thus a very tall, thin man, was dubbed 'Pull through' from his testified resemblance to the piece of cord and brass known as a pull-through, and used to clean the rifle. 'Snowball' was the owner of a bullet head covered with very, very fair, pale, straw-coloured hair, and when he lay tucked in bed with the bedclothes above his nose and only his fair hair showing, he really did resemble a large snowball. The cognomen 'Snowflake' on the other hand, was a piece of irony which was appreciated and enjoyed by the owner of the name as much as by any one else, for he was a native of Trinidad and dusky as could be. 'Darkey' had spent a good many years in Mexico, and had become very swarthy in the time.

'Somebody's darling' had fair, curly hair, blue eyes, pink cheeks, and a bow mouth and was aged eighteen. 'Charlie Chaplin' shortened to 'Charlie' and 'Chappie' owed his name to his walk, or, more truthfully, to his feet which were inclined to be distant with one another. 'Farmer Garge' was a bluff and hearty, beef-and-beer, John-Bull type of man with a big, red face, and as much mutton-chop as the Army allows.

I am afraid I was responsible for one nickname. There was one little boy in the ward who simply wouldn't talk. All we could charm from him was monosyllables, a few smiles, and many blushes. 'Now, Magpie,' I said one day when I went to make his bed, 'talkative as ever I suppose.' And 'Magpie' stuck to him. After he had left the ward the other men told me he had been accustomed to declare himself a woman hater! [he was aged eighteen] and one thing he didn't mind about up the line was that there were no women. On protestation he admitted – oh, balm to my 'satiable vanity! – he didn't mind 'our sister,' she 'wasn't half a bad sort, that she wasn't.'

Then we had 'Dormouse' who had a truly voracious appetite for sleep, would sleep like the Seven Sleepers all night, and then doze like an octogenarian all day. 'Rip Van Winkle' was the name bestowed on a man of similar tendency in another ward. 'Tiny' and 'Bantam' were playful pieces of irony, for both were Grenadiers whose toes came to the bottom of the bed. Ironical, too, was the designation of 'Lightning' to a bulky, leisurely moving man who, according to the consensus of general ward opinion, was 'too slow to catch cold.'

One night, we had brought in two boys who came straight from the trenches bringing with them thick shocks of hair and semi-patriarchal beards.

'Well, sister, have you any one you would like me to see?' asked the divisional major of a nurse, when, a little later, he did his rounds. He referred, of course, to any anxious eases.

'Yes,' said she, interpreting his words quite literally and naughtily pointing out the two boys. 'Here are Robinson Crusoe and his man Friday.'

Both joined the Major in a broad grin and 'Crusoe' and 'Friday' they remained so long as they stayed with us.

Certain nicknames are given as a matter of course – Jock to Scotchmen, Geordie to North country-men, Taffy to Welshmen, Pat to Irishmen, 'Aussy' to Australians or otherwise 'we from Kangerland,' 'Dads' to any old – or rather should I say 'old-looking' man, – 'Sonny' and 'Chikko' to 'youngsters,' 'Boy' to all and sundry. A man too, is often addressed by the name of the district from which he hails. 'Now, Lancashire [or Warwick – or Gloucester, etc.], muck in. D'yer think yer a blooming sergeant-major?'

Nicknames spring up rife in these happy-go-lucky, soldier gatherings. The main thing is to possess one, for a nickname is a sign of good fellowship, *bon camaraderie,* popularity, a sign that the owner is admitted to the *coterie* of pals, a sign that he is 'in the swim.'

Chapter XII
'Blighty'

'GET THE TEMPERATURE down and then...' The Medical Officer pauses significantly and smiles. Whereat the patient grins broadly at him and at the sister, and, as they move to the next bed, his thoughts have already landed in England.

A couple of days later, probably, he receives his tickets, and the congratulations of the ward. 'Two tickets,' he is warned by the waggish one of the party, 'one to go with and one to come back with.'

'That's all right, Sour Grapes. So long as I get there, I'm willing to come back and give old Fritz one in the neck, for doing it down on me now. What would you give me for my chance of England, Home and Huddersfield?', glancing up at the suspended tickets.

Meantime his 'going-away costume' is stowed into

the bottom of his locker – pyjamas, warm undershirt, bed socks, helmet and muffler. Were he a 'sitting case' with a slight G.S.W. of the arm or head, or a 'sick' case with a slight disease of the heart or debility, he would have a full, khaki, clothing kit drawn from the stores, this kit being supplemented if necessary, with an extra muffler, or an extra pair of woollen mittens or similar comfort, from the Red Cross Stores.

These kits are put in readiness almost immediately, for a patient has often been warned, and evacuated within an hour of receiving tickets. Some cases are occasionally given tickets but their evacuation is delayed for a time owing to their not being in a fit condition to travel. The tickets are, however, given them for the excellent mental effect their possession has upon the patient, and consequently in great measure upon his progress.

There are three headings which a medical officer uses when filling in tickets for England cases. Each patient, as most people know, receive two tickets resembling luggage labels, and bearing in addition to the name of the hospital or the number of the CCS. – casualty clearing station – the patient's name, number, and regiment, together with the date and the name of the hospital ship by which the patient travels.

On the reverse side of the ticket are chronicled the diagnosis, any treatment required *en route,* the man's age, total service, service in France and religion, – all items of information sometimes required. If anything additional is to be forwarded, such as a history of the case, a medical case sheet, an X-ray photograph, etc., it is enclosed in a special envelope. Certain cases are indicated in a particular manner, e.g., nephritics have a yellow label distinctive of nephritis, and hence ensuring a 'nephritic diet' *en route.*

Each ticket has a further inscription in block letters, 'C Sitting', 'L.T.B.' and 'L.T.A.' 'C Sitting' means a seat on the ambulance car, a seat on board ship, unless, of course, the length of the journey demands a cot, and a seat on the train and ambulance car in England. It is also further understood that the man, after inspection on embarking, needs no special attention beyond the usual nursing care and supervision.

'Lying train B' patients are stretcher cases throughout the journey. They are brought from the ward on a stretcher, have a stretcher place on the ambulance car, a cot on board, and lying accommodation to the hospital in England.

'Lying train A' patients are conveyed in similar fashion to those marked 'L.T.B.' except that being

THE 'BLIGHTY' SMILE – AN L.T.A. CASE

more serious cases, they have the best positioned cots on board. The greatest number of cots, by the way, are swing cots.

Helpless cases – one is thankful to say they are infrequent – have a red cross diagonally across their tickets, and the word 'helpless' printed in block at the foot of the ticket. Why are such cases sent? Because the patients get to a stage when the longing for 'Blighty' is retarding their progress, the bed is wanted and the particular case is tedious, and requires long home nursing as distinctive from A.S. nursing, e.g. baths, electrical massage, certain prolonged treatments.

'All L.T.B.s due at the point at 10.30, sister. Ambulance train in,' comes the message; 9.30 now, no time to lose. Dressing sheets, bandages, lotions, cotton wool, drums are brought out, instruments and lotion bowls boiled or fired, and one sets to work to do the necessary dressings, and make the wounds as comfortable and safe as possible. The wounds finished, one helps to dress wounded lying patients, and inspects the sitting cases. This inspection is most necessary, for 'men are but children of a larger growth,' which was just another way of saying that men are as irresponsible as naughty boys.

Thus the masculine sex, as a class, has a rooted objection to fastening the neck of its shirt, preferring on a bitterly cold, January day to invite pneumonia as ardently as any foolish flapper with the veriest V-shaped blouse. It delights too, in hurrying into its nether garments and making a brave show to the world in well-pulled-down khaki, brightly burnished buttons and well-rolled puttees, even though its cardigan is guiltless of a button, and its socks are only fit for the waste-wool bag.

Finally, all are fixed and rounded up, and the 'sitting cases' potter about first on one impatient leg then the other, like so many little boys keen to be off to a party, and privately thinking no doubt that we are frightfully fussy when we insist on every string and buckle being fastened.

Good-byes and handshakes are over, and they troop out in charge of an orderly who takes them to the point. I stand at the tent door half a minute, and wave to them as they look back. Poor lads, bruised in the battle, heads bandaged, arms in slings, shuffling feet in great trench slippers, limping footsteps aided by a couple of walking sticks – poor boys! But in England there is rest and peace, and time to pause and take breath . . . I turn to help stretcher bearers and orderly move the lying cases on to the stretchers, and to see blankets tucked snugly round feet and throat, treasure bag tucked under the pillow, and any little needful accessory supplied, – a jaconet-covered pillow on which to rest a wounded arm, a small pillow under the shoulder, or, as has sometimes happened, to tie or to bandage in place a little ring pillow we have specially made to relieve pressure on an injured surface.

Then an onslaught on the beds, this bedding and mattress to the fumigator, that fracture board to be scrubbed with cresolis, this bedstead to be carbolised, this mackintosh sheet to be carbolised, these bandages to be soaked in a disinfectant and then to go to the wash, this cradle to be wiped with strong carbolic, these beds to be re-made with clean linen. And so we speed the parting guest, and make ready for the newcomers.

Ambulance train No. X is drawn up in a siding. Standing there on a curve of the rails its fourteen coaches all absolutely uniform in height, shape and colour – khaki with the Red Cross – it looks from the distance ridiculously like a toy, a child's plaything rather than the meeting place of hopelessness and hope, despair and thankfulness, sorrow and joy, tragedy and comedy.

The train is ready to receive its load, beds made, pillows freshly tossed, clean linen laid out, the cooks already preparing the dinner, the theatre absolutely ready for any emergency operation, the dispensary looking spick and span, the orderlies putting in readiness sundry drinks, the sisters walking up and down supervising, seeing to any deficiencies and adding any little touch of brightness or extra comfort to the wards. The Medical Officer in charge of the train, and the Train Officer are on the platform ready to see all patients placed on board. The ambulance cars arrive, two or three at a time. It is wonderful how steadily the stream of cars is maintained, avoiding both congestion and the slightest loss of time. The cars are drawn close to the door of the compartment, the stretchers drawn out, lifted on level with the floor of the carriage, drawn in, then raised to the bed which is either at the level of the ordinary compartment seat or, in case of the upper berth, on level with the smaller and lower luggage rack found in an ordinary train. This unloading from car and loading on train is done extremely deftly, most expeditiously, and with the minimum of movement. Of course, the nature of the cases determine in great measure the length of time taken to load a train, but three hundred cases have often been entrained in less than an hour.

The train loaded, it is interesting to walk along it while the M.O. in charge checks numbers, signs documents, and goes through the usual formalities with the Train Officer. Except that all the passengers are khaki-clad, and most of them are bandaged, the compartments containing the sitting cases look much like those of any other train. Here are men spreading an overcoat preparatory to playing cards, there are men unfurling newspapers – a couple of days old – and flicking over the leaves of magazines. Here are men fidgeting about ventilators and fussing about windows. Here is a luggage agitator, misplacing and getting excited about his luggage – all contained in a 'Sister-Susie' bag – just as effectually as though he had Saratoga, cabin trunks and portmanteaux galore.

The lying cases or 'lyers' as they often call themselves, clad in great coats and pyjamas, are shorn of their coat and put to bed. Some go into compartments arranged like a four-bunk cabin, the two seats forming two beds, and in place of the customary luggage racks, two more beds. Other coaches are not divided into compartments, but have tiers of beds arranged longitudinally with the train, and thus make a ward of thirty-six or forty beds. Most beds are woven on the hammock principle, and hence are softer and more comfortable than if made of wood and springs. All have conveniently placed straps near them for support. Bells, too, are handy, in case a summons for assistance is necessary. These bells, however, are extremely infrequently used, as orderlies, sisters and medical officers are constantly on duty, passing almost incessantly up and down. An average train staff might consist of forty or fifty orderlies, two staff nurses, a sister acting-matron, one doctor, or two doctors, with the rank of captain and a major in charge. There is also the kitchen staff, for hundreds of dinners, teas, suppers, breakfasts, and diets must be cooked in the spotlessly clean, beautifully tidy, little kitchen.

A coach provides for the nursing staff, mess room, tiny writing-room and sleeping quarters. One compartment is allotted as living – or, rather, sleeping-quarters to each two nurses, the compartment seat providing the bed, the luggage rack the wardrobe, and the rest of the compartment everything else necessary. Somewhat circumscribed in area, of course, but what would you? It is better than a dug-out, and one is not hypercritical of bed on active service, especially after a long journey, which has, on occasion, lasted thirty hours, and during which time there has only been, exclusive of hurried meal times, an hour off-duty for resting.

Life for the hospital staff of a train is apt to be a pretty strenuous affair with peeps of a *dolce far niente* if the train happens to need repairs. Should the repairs take a long time, the nursing staff is drafted for duty to an adjacent hospital.

Here are extracts from a diary of a 'train sister':

July 2. Loaded at 8 a.m. Arrived E—— 2 a.m. Back to G—— by midnight. Straightened the wards and slept on the return journey.

July 3. Loaded and arrived B—— by 9 a.m. Back to F—— by 6 p.m. Take on four hundred and sixty stretcher cases.

July 4. Arrive R——. Left at noon for V——. Five hundred and sixty cases, two hundred of whom were Germans.

July 5. From V—— to E—— then back to V——, which left at midnight.

July 6. Arrived C— at 7 a.m. Unloaded and at

V—— again at 1.30 p.m. Arrive E—— at 11 p.m.

July 7. Awoke at A—— *en route* for D——. Arrive at 11 a.m.

July 17. Arrive S—— at 9.30 a.m. Town criers telling inhabitants to be in their cellars by 8 p.m. What a curfew!

Aug. 1. Left 4 a.m. gathering patients at A——, F—— and D——. Total, five hundred cases and weather very hot. Arrive at E—— on the coast. Gorgeous.

Aug. 13. Loaded rather late to-night. Up all night.

Aug. 14. Arrive R—— 8 a.m. Bought some bread, fresh butter and fruit. Left 11 a.m. Arrive L—— 8 p.m.

Aug. 15. In L—— all day. Went for a walk, and passing through a cemetery, found there the grave of 'Jimmy Anzac' whom I had nursed in Malta. Poor, poor boy, and what a strange chance I should find his grave.

Sep. 3. Loaded at A——, B——, R——, on to B——. Arrived 11 p.m.

Sep. 4. Off again at 8.30. Same journey as yesterday. Arrived back at 9 p.m. Concertina part of train damaged. In garage for repairs.

Sep. 6. Left for L——. Bored with rations so made cakes for tea on the way. How good they tasted!

Sep. 7. Made arrangements for more permanent cross over Jimmy's grave. Off loaded to B——. Very big load, third of which Germans.

H.M. Hp. S. D . . . lies straining at her moorings, a great, big, white beauty with the distinctive green band and the three red crosses – one amidships, one to stem, one to stern – painted on her bows, and above, on deck, the great red crosses to be lighted at night. Sailors pass leisurely to and fro in the detached, desultory manner that sailors have. A batch of R.A.M.C. orderlies stand idling by a heap of brown blankets. A couple of sisters lean over the taffrail lazily gossiping. Not a medical officer is to be seen.

There she lies, as idle as a painted ship upon a painted ocean.

Then the snorting of an engine, and the thunder of heavy wheels, and round the curve of the railway comes a long khaki-coloured hospital train. The ship immediately becomes a bustle of activity. Stretcher bearers run down the gangway to the stretchers waiting in readiness on the platform, for this particular ship happens to be moored alongside the railway station of a great French port.

The ship's medical officers come down to receive their cases from the care of the train's officers. Any patient who has been ill on the train journey and is liable to be adversely affected by the sea-journey is detained for a few days, and sent into a hospital which adjoins the station, and which has been housed in the premises of the gare, the buffets, waiting-rooms, *douane,* etc. Here a patient who has had, perhaps, a haemorrhage brought on by the jolting of the train can recuperate, and have a further rest before proceeding on his journey.

The cases are sorted, the heavier ones, i.e., those needing most assistance, being detailed to the top decks so as to be more quickly got off the boat in case of accident. The lighter cases, i.e., those able to help themselves, go to the lower decks and in the downstairs wards. Cases possible to haemorrhage or to require dressing are put into lower berths, while bad travelling cases, e.g., those with abdominal injuries or with gastric trouble are given the best placed berths with the least amount of rocking attendant. Even spinal cases are carried, – and carried most successfully too, – splinted from head to foot, of course, and subject to every precaution and care throughout the journey. Splints, by the way, are quite freely used when dressing the cases for England, not merely for fractures, but wherever jolting or movement of a limb is likely to cause pain.

The walking cases, meantime, with huge Blighty smiles which broaden in superlative fashion as they greet us, have ensconced themselves on board, and have either found cushy chairs or seats and magazines, – which they show little inclination as yet to read, – or are watching the stretcher cases taken on board and sent by lift to the deck specified. These lifts combine the maximum utility with the minimum of space and elaboration. They consist of a grooved wooden support to take the ends of the stretcher with a webbed surface underlying the stretcher itself and their raising or lowering is worked by a belt.

All patients duly aboard and comfortably settled, tea is served. Then comes a walk round the ship which has not yet started her journey on account of certain sailing restrictions. One peeps in at the dispensary with its lotions and potions, its ungents and palliatives; then another peep at the operating theatre, a beautiful, white room fitted with two tables for emergency work, and, fortunately, not often required – unless in case of a long journey or in a heavy rush of patients.

The open door of the 'wireless room' shows a small cabin where all night long an operator will do his little bit towards ensuring a safe journey for the poor, broken boys aboard. One eyes somewhat more than inquisitively the stacked rafts, the open boats and the two motor launches, the latter known as Puffing Billy and Snorting Lizzie, Lizzie being the one into which the wireless operator and his batteries are to go in case of necessity.

Many people who realise how enormous is the task of moving wounded will have marvelled at the proportionately small number of casualties when hospital ships have been torpedoed. This is undoubtedly due to the fact that every member of the staff of the ship knows his or her duty in such circumstances, each has been drilled in his or her particular work, and routine, and the realisation of the importance of that duty have done the rest.

So far as preparedness goes, it is somewhat amusing to note that many of the nursing sisters when on long journeys used to sleep in their swimming costumes.

The autumn afternoon has waned in a purple-red splendour and darkness falls. Supper has been served, and we walk round each ward. We are not carrying officers on this journey, and the L.T.A. boys have the officers' cots, placed in what was formerly the ladies' drawing-room. The lights are shaded and the little cream curtains drawn where requested. 'Cushy, sister,' we are assured, 'if it warn't for the island at the other side of the water, I could stay here for the duration.'

Down below, the sitting cases are going to bed in a big ward having tiers of beds arranged on metal supporting rods. The effect is, in a way, somewhat grotesque for the arrangement reminds one of so many tins of cakes in the cooling room of a bakery. On the way to the deck, we see through an open door into the engine room, with four huge boilers like Brobdignagian sparking plugs.

Above we find an unexpected shower of rain. Drawn alongside our hospital ship is a leave boat, dull grey in colour, and with decks roofed in tarpaulin, whose wet surface brightly glistens in the light of a naptha flare.

On the quay is a queue of khaki boys, jesting and happy, wholly disregardful of so slight a thing as the weather. Their leave papers examined they run up the gangway, a hunched figure with 'humpy' well-hitched on to their shoulders, and with heart, no doubt, as light as their pack is heavy. The dark-roofed ship swallows them as effectually as a tank does, and we think

of the dim phantom with her war-worn freight steal-
ing through the grey waters. Good luck, boys, and a
good leave.

The rain ceases as unexpectedly as it came, and
by the time we put out to sea, a young moon shines
benignly on us, promising a smooth passage. A good
passage we have, too, and a quiet uneventful night so
far as the nursing is concerned.

'Sister, where are we, and is it really morning?'

'Lying off Netley, and it is half-past seven.'

'So we're across. No tin fishes.'

'Of course not.'

'And I haven't been seasick.'

'Of course not.'

'And we're all glad to leave IT behind for awhile.'

'OF – COURSE – NOT.'

There is only one form of repartee in the Tommy
Atkins vocabulary to meet that remark, and it comes –

'I DON'T think, sister.'

Four trains are drawn up at the English port to take
away the cases from our hospital ship, and those from
another which has come in alongside us. The first
train is filled quickly with the more slightly-wounded
sitting-cases, and is sent a short journey so as to be
back in time to fill up again with the last patients left

on board. The heaviest cases are also sent the shortest possible journey consistent with the best nursing and medical conditions, so as to eliminate, as much as possible, travelling and jolting.

Once the train starts, heads are stretched and necks craned to catch a glimpse of the land of our many thoughts, and occasional dreams, while we were 'out there.' The morning sun pours floods of light on the reds and russets, the golds and bronzes, the browns and dark greens of the wooded copses. We catch fleeting glimpses of red-roofed farms, trim, well-built dwelling houses, orderly little towns, and – adorable little English children! Ours is a country worth fighting for, worth dying for, worth being maimed for. A funny thing – love of one's native land. We who have endured heartbreaking scenes in those hospital wards in Normandy look away from one another now and blink very hard.

Otherwise, we bid fair to make fools of ourselves soon.

Chapter XIII
Heroes in their Carpet Slippers

'WHAT ARE THE men like?' a military nurse is very often asked. 'Do they make good patients?'

Well, all the eulogies that have been showered on them, all the epithets and superlatives that have been rained on them, are but deserved. Splendid, magnificent, superb, they certainly are, heroes undoubtedly. But no man is a hero to his valet, and no man will permit himself to be a hero to his nurse. Homeric and epic they may be, but that fact they jealously guard from their nurse. Hence it is the homely human side we see. It is their trivial weaknesses, their little peculiarities, their big rough-diamond virtues we know. We see heroism shorn of its rifle, bayonet, and shrapnel helmet, and dressed in loose 'blues' and carpet slippers.

Their brave deeds they persistently hide from us. 'And what did you do to win the M.M.?' one boy was asked. 'Ah only fetcht a man hin,' he almost surlily replied, his averted face plainly showing a disinclination for further conversation.

Later, when our little blandishments had worn down his dourness, he thawed enough to explain that it took eleven hours to bring in the man, that he was 'as good an officer as ever put two feet into shoes,' that both of them were wounded, and craved for water, and that he had had to drag or carry the officer every inch of the way. Think of it! Eleven hours, almost a waking day, from breakfast to dinner-time, and every minute an exquisite torture of pain, perpetual suspense, and concentrated effort. But that was nothing to talk to 'sister' about. 'Ah only fetcht a man hin.'

With regard to decorations, they are modesty *in excelsis*. Although whispers pass round to other patients that another has a decoration, – and let me add their consequent respect and envy, – yet the owner himself never alludes to it, – he might be suspected of 'swank.' One man I congratulated on the possession of the M.M. 'Oh!' deprecatingly, 'only an apology for the V.C. But.' – with a little smile, – 'my wife will be pleased.'

In the earlier, more leisurely days of the war we used to prefer the boys while in the wards to wear their ribbons, the South African, the D.C.M., the M.M., pinned to their pyjama coats, but the modest wretches had a habit of taking off either of the two latter and hiding it when our backs were turned. They seemed to dread the other men regarding the wearing of it as their conceit rather than our wishes.

As patients, 'our boys' are perpetually amazing. They will silently endure agonies from wounds and dressings, and yet groan and even howl when one removes a little adhesive plaster. They will tolerate stoically a shrapnel-ridden left leg, and yell from the further end of the ward to have a pillow or a piece of cotton wool moved under the heel of the right.

Their sangfroid is tremendous. One smoked a pipe half-an-hour before he died, others one has caught smoking a cigarette within a few minutes of coming from the theatre. 'Oh, I'm going great guns, sister,' said a little boy with an amputation of the left leg. 'As a matter of fact,' went on the dreadful boy, 'I think it will be a good idea to cut the other leg off to the same length. Then I could join the bantams. Don't look so shocked, sister.'

Another boy smoked a cigarette (bless the shade

of Sir Walter Raleigh!) and joked to a sister who was holding up for him a picture paper the while his leg was being amputated below the knee. Stovaine was used, and the operation was very successful.

The way the boys accept matters is simply marvellous. One was taken into the theatre to have a minor operation to his leg. Matters, however, were found to be so much worse than had been evident that it was a case of amputating the leg or letting the boy die. Naturally, the leg was taken off, and when I came on duty at night it was to be told to the boy, who was still under the influence of the anaesthetic and did not, of course, know of the amputation.

I dreaded having to tell him. Each of the several times I went to feel his pulse, look at his dressing, etc., he was asleep, so next morning when the lights were fully turned up I went in trepidation to wash him and make his bed. To my astonishment he knew: he had awakened during the night, seen the bedclothes turned back – a plan we always adopt to facilitate the immediate detection of any possible haemorrhage – had realised what had happened, and quietly gone to sleep again without my knowing he had been awake. 'Of course, it is a great grief to me,' he remarked, 'but' – very charmingly – 'I have been long enough here to know that whatever any one did for me is for the best.'

Winter nights in hospital are the most domesticated times. It is then that our warriors from the trenches completely unbend. Wind and snow are lashing outside, but the tents are tightly laced, and blankets hung over the drawn entrance flaps. After supper gramophones, dominoes, cards, and games are put away, and often the up-patients will crowd round the stove, when somehow the conversation invariably turns to the old and young folks at home.

Then each newcomer takes his photograph from his 'Sister Susie bag,' while older patients sit round ready on the slightest pretext to do the same, although we have already seen their photographs. On each, one makes adequate comments while occasionally having to cudgel one's brain for appropriate and pleasing remark.

'That's the eldest girl. She is thirteen, and has just won a scholarship.'

'Really! She looks very clever. And what beautiful hair!'

'That's the youngest, – ten months. I haven't seen him. That's my wife and family.'

'Very capable woman I should think.'

'Ah, she is that. Makes all the children's clothes. She made those frocks they have on.'

'Indeed!' one says in a tone of surprise sufficient to be gratifying, though one glance at the delineated garments is enough to advertise the brave little effort blatantly, and, in a way, pathetically. Later, demands are made on our admiration on behalf of little girls in white dresses standing by pedestals adorned with baskets of flowers, little boys dressed *à la Fauntleroy,* with hand on head of a shaggy mongrel with not an atom of breeding, but quite evidently a faithful, great-hearted, doggy thing, entirely lovable. And lastly there is 'Me, taken in France.'

'Me, taken in France' is invariably very glossy, very shiny, full-length, post card size, three for a franc. A Frenchman taken in this style twirls his moustache, throws out his chest, puts on a *pour-ma-patrie* expression, and looks quite in the picture. But a British gunner sitting gingerly on a Louis Quatorze chair in front of a Watteauesque terrace, with peacock sailing along – a British gunner with firmly planted feet and hands, and a very conscious, almost defiant, expression peculiar to his photographed state, presents a sight, which to say the least, is somewhat amusingly incongruous. Still we mete out a semi-critical admiration, the critical suggestion being hinted at to ensure the genuineness of the admiration, and to remove any doubts that 'sister's gettin' at yer.'

From the 'Sister Susie' bags, too, come little souvenirs – a rosary picked up on the battlefield, the nose of a shell, a trench ring, a watch-chain made from flattened bullets, and, often wrapped in a piece of bandage, the fragments of shrapnel 'that bowled me over.' This shrapnel is twisted into a piece of bandage and tied to the arm on the wounded side of the body when the man leaves the theatre, or it is sometimes laid on the stretcher and tied to his bedstead on the corresponding side. In the great majority of cases the men prize this shrapnel enormously and have it made into a rough 'charm' for sister or wife or sweetheart; in a few other cases, 'No, sister: I don't want it: had quite enough of it.'

During the July push several German helmets were brought down as souvenirs. I remember one man, with wound dressed and waiting for the Blighty train, seated outside the tent, asking me to admire his 'millinery,' a Prussian helmet, round which he had placed a string of dandelions.

Yes, they are cheery, happy, casual sort of rascals, content, so long as they get their 'Blighty tickets and a bit of furlough,' to come back again and take up the game of 'dodging Fritz and Co.,' and strafing the 'blinking old sossidge eaters.'

Chapter XIV
Red Cross Needlework

An Appreciation

'SEVEN CASES MARKED for England, five "Lying Train B," and two "C Sitting." I had better go to the Red Cross Stores and get their clothes,' – their 'trousseau' or 'going-away dress,' the men usually call the outfit.

As I leave the tent, I make a mental note of what I want. Seven shirts, five pairs of pyjamas, five pairs of bed-socks, five woollen helmets, seven pairs of cuffs, or mittens, and two thick scarves, since November weather in the Channel is too raw and bleak to take risks. Then, too, I had better replenish our stock of bath-gloves and 'Dorothy bags' – more commonly known among the men as 'Sister Susie bags' – our small pillows, milk covers, and nightingales.

What a godsend to us is the tiny, tightly packed

room known as the Red Cross Stores! To convey what its comforts have meant to the maimed, bruised men they have clothed, to realise what it means to have such a supply to draw from, no human words are in any way adequate. The imagination might succeed a little better, though even then it would fall as far short of the reality as a child's attempted conception of a billion of anything.

We nurses *know* how much the gifts and comforts are appreciated, and we would emphatically assure all the women who have associated themselves with the distaff part of war work that every garment or article made, earned from some painracked man his grateful, heartfelt, though inarticulate, thanks. Every stitch they have made meant a few minutes' greater comfort – and correspondingly less pain – from an aching body tortured on our behalf, for our defence and our birthrights. It is in no way a far-fetched statement to say that some garments – such as pneumonia jackets and cholera belts – have prolonged a man's life. Many needlewomen have deplored and belittled their share in the war's work; they have deprecated their efforts because these have not necessitated the donning of a uniform and the complete upheaval of their former life. If they would imagine what the comfort and warmth of their nice, smooth, home-knitted socks are to cold, chilblained feet, if they could see the men snuggling head and frost-nipped ears into their cosy Balaclavas, if they could witness – as we nurses have done – how a small jaconet-covered pillow, placed under the scapula of a man with his arm in an extension, has secured for the poor man a good night's rest, there would be no more deprecating talk, no more half-sighing comments that 'I don't seem to be doing much. I'm only a Sister Susie.' Be proud you are a 'Sister Susie.' You are doing some of the most valuable war service. The comfort supplying department is as necessary to the Army Medical Service as the Commissariat or the Clothing Department is to the army in the field. The fighting forces are infinitely glad of the existence of Sister Susies and their nimble fingers.

There are two sets of people I should like to take for half-an-hour into the Red Cross Stores of any E.F. Hospital. One is our fighting men and the other is the women slackers. I should like the men to see those many, many garments, each bearing tangible proof of myriads of kind thoughts towards them and aching desires to help them, sometimes, doubtless, with hopes and fears, dumb sorrow and poignant anxiety woven into every loop of sock and meshed muffler. The slackers would, I hope, be shamed by those many evidences of tireless industry and by the unselfishness those garments epitomise into going and doing likewise.

Look at this scarf. It was worked by frail fingers, the unevenness of the knitting shows that – done by a child or an old lady. No, not by a child, the scarf is too long for a child's patience and concentration. Not only are the kind old knitter's hands frail, her eyesight is failing, too. Here the dropped stitches have been picked up not quite correctly, here the matching of the wool is not accurate. But perhaps the latter was due to the limitations of the village shop, for one feels certain from the quality of the wool that the scarf was knitted by an old villager with not too many pennies to spare.

Here is a bundle of neatly hemmed calico handkerchiefs labelled 'Blackcote Girls' School, Std. II.' Std. II sounds very juvenile, and evidently there underlies a Herculean effort. One conjures up a vision of curly dark and golden heads, earnestly bent over the squares of calico, as chubby two-inch-long fingers laboriously push hot and sticky needles through the calico, and occasionally into the pink flesh, in valiant attempts to do their baby share of the war-work.

Last night one of 'my boys' died. He had gas gangrene, and he cried continually, 'Where's my lavender bag, sister? My wound does smell so.' I heaped some lavender bags into a piece of muslin and slipped it under his top pillow, besides hanging other satchets round him wherever possible. There are dozens of other boys who appreciate the lavender bags, boys who are nauseated by the smell of their wound whilst it is being dressed. For their sake it is good to see a new consignment, bunches of half a dozen sprigs of lavender, the stalks serving as handle, and the blooms shielded with a muslin cover caught with ribbon, an excellent time-saving, handy, convenient method of sending out the lavender.

The neat idea of the bags is typical of the dispatch with which all the work in the stores has been done. Any woman interested in needlework could not fail to note with admiring approval how cleverly garments and comforts have been designed to obtain simplicity of making, convenience of wearing, and the greatest economy of effort in their production. She need only look at the cut and the putting together of each article to see that they have been planned thoroughly well and ingeniously before ever the scissors were introduced to them, planned so as to make the best use of the material and the shortest use of the worker's time. They are sensible, useful, got-together-quickly garments, that are a credit to the needlewomen who have so efficiently made them.

Strict economy, too, one notes. Look at this wash-rag, ingeniously made by knitting up the torn-off selvedge discarded from lengths of calico! And these slippers made from linoleum and scraps of strong cloth.

Occasionally women may have felt a little depressed as the conscience-salvers recited the ancient tale of socks with 'no shape,' and shirts with 'neckbands as large as waist-belts.' It is an immense pity if they were adversely influenced by these remarks, if they allowed the ridicule to diminish their energies.

Personally, I have never seen any such imaginary garment as the conscience-salvers love to cite and at which they love to sneer. Among many thousands of shirts, socks, pyjamas and bed-jackets, I have never seen one but was not very well made. Certainly I have never seen one garment of which we have not been able to make excellent use. So all the needlewomen who sew for 'our boys' via the Red Cross, can rest assured that they do their 'bit,' a bit that is most grate-fully appreciated, and they can continue to ply their needle and thread into wool and cotton and flannel, and stitch, stitch, stitch for the boys who have gone forth to fight.

NOTE

The above was written in the autumn of 1915. Since then we have in some branches made less call on the Red Cross. For example, pyjamas and stockings for England cases are drawn from the quartermaster's stores, but for the many needlework, and the countless little extra comforts which the Red Cross supply, all we nurses, on behalf of the 'boys,' are deeply grateful and extremely appreciative.

Chapter XV

Our Concerts

An O.A.S. concert is a much more exciting affair than any one at home would ever imagine. We come from far and near to a concert. When the chairs and forms are filled – which happens all too soon – we sit on billiard tables and overturned buckets, and even on the floor. The fortunate part of the overflow audience outside, stand on ration boxes and look in at the window, while the unfortunate part roams up and down, hearing a snatch of the performance here and another there, and living in hopes of the time when some cramped mortal may become tired of hanging on by the toes of one foot to a three-inch square of ration box, and will give up his place to the wandering snapper-up of greatly considered trifles.

The front of the orchestra stalls looks like the

THE D.D.M.S. PAYS HIS OFFICIAL VISIT OF INSPECTION, ON WHAT IS COMMONLY KNOWN AS 'WIND-UP', OR 'EYEWASH', DAY

pool of Bethesda. For hither have been brought those lying cases which can be carried, patients stretched in invalid chairs, boys with much bandaged legs or great bundles, representing feet, tenderly placed on another chair before them.

Artistes assure us that we are 'topping audiences' for none of us are *blasé* and none of us are bored. We all join enthusiastically in the choruses, and it is quite amusing to have bandaged boys, choleric colonels, dashing majors, gentle nurses and high-spirited V.A.D.s firmly assuring every one in general and no one in particular:

> *'Left, left,*
> *I'd a jolly good home*
> *And I left.'*

or sighing against

> *'The day when I'll be going down*
> *That long, long trail with you.'*

Poor boys! Some who have sung those words with us have already gone down the trail.

The staging effects are a positive triumph of adaptation. The footlights are in biscuit tins, the hospital gear provides endless props and wardrobes. 'The Bushrangers,' for example, were in hospital shirts, red ties, riding-breeches, leggings, boots and 'dinkum' hats. A rustic invariably appears in khaki trousers, tied under the knee with string, cotton shirt from hospital acting as smock, and one of the familiar red ties.

A West Indian band delighted us one night to more, and ever more, encores...and their instruments? All home-made, one from a cigar-box, one from a tin tobacco box, one from a tin basin, and one – of the flute variety – from a piece of thin metal tubing.

The programmes usually assure us that an 'egg-proof curtain will be lowered repeatedly during the performance. The artistes believe that prevention is better than cure.' We are often respectfully asked, too, to keep our seats and 'maintain a sympathetic silence until the conclusion of the performance. Several doctors are included in the audience.'

'The Management,' said one notice, 'has arranged for the provision of beds in the Medical Hut for any members of the audience who contract sleeping sickness.

Wigs – by Jove!
Songs – by the way.

Costumes – by inspection of the Censor.

Jewellery – by the Sixpence-ha'penny Bazaar.

Entr'acte – Descendez au bar.

The programmes are cheerily informal affairs with a lack of big type that would send a leading lady or an actor manager into a fit of apoplexy.

Here is a typical one:

PART I

1. We commence.
2. Smith asks Romeo for a row.
3. Brown wants to sing – so let him.
4. Jones bursts into song.

    The audience will probably burst into tears.

5. Robinson will oblige.
6. Smithson insists and won't be kept back.
7. Sketch – Some lorry inspection.

[It was.]

PART II

1. Robinson with a smile and a kit bag.
2. The Animated Forceps throws things about, including himself.
3. Encore Smith.
4. Jones tours an old-fashioned town.

5. Brown gives a pathetic recitation about four 'CO.' sparking plugs.
6. Smithson refuses to wait any longer.
7. We must be patriotic to conclude.

The 'advertisements' give playful little digs at all and sundry. The sergeant in charge of the clothing stores finds he has a space wherein he is described as –

> 'Dealer in cast-off clothing.
> Old boots collected.
> Get a chit.'

Harrison and Williamson, who happen to have had a good deal of night work with transport, are described in another square as

> 'FURNITURE REMOVERS
> The Moonlighters' Friends.'

The Railway Transport Section are, in another space, made into a Limited Liability Company who are

> 'TOURIST AGENTS
> Tours arranged to the British Isles.'

One announcement which the boys much appreciated, for they have a great taste, – if I may say so, – for alcoholic jokes is:

> 'Rye and Barley's Whiskey.
>   TRY ONE.
>   TRY ANOTHER.
>   TRY ANOTHER.
>   TRY ANOTHER.
> Feel better, what?'

This, for some reason or other, sent the boys into paroxysms of laughter. The masculine sense of humour is, at times, a little puzzling.

Chapter XVI

English as She is Spoken
(With the B.E.F.)

'APRÈS LA GUERRE finit, après la guerre napoo,' he softly sang, laboriously scratching away at the black box which had contained the gift chocolate from the West Indian Colonies. He was removing the paint with a pin, thus showing the tin beneath, and forming a design of his Oxford and Bucks badge and the R.A.M.C. twisted serpent. Engraving these boxes had very much of a vogue in our wards at the time, and some beautifully artistic effects had been the result.

'Have a dekko, draftie. Très bon, isn't it? This one is for sister as a souvenir. The first one I did I'm going to send to Blighty for the youngsters. But it'll have to wait until I go out of hospital. All my pay-days have gone West since I've been here swinging the lead. Alley, toot swee,' he continues clearing the table as I come through the tunnel with the medicine basket, 'line up for the rum ration, boys. Runner, sister?'

'Please.'

''Ere yare, matey, bonne santé, bonne année, bonne nuit,' as he offers the first dose.

'Merci boaco, merci cocoa,' elegantly retorts the recipient.

'Ser nay fair reang,' with a shrug, not to be outdone in politeness nor in knowledge of the French language. 'Taffy's getting the wind up, sister, when he sees you laying hands on the saucy sal,' otherwise the sodii sal.

'Buck up and drink it. Bon for the troops,' Taffy is urged. 'You're too slow to catch cold. If you want to linger longer in quaffing the cup, go to a hestaminay. Oh, sister,' in terrible reproach, 'I thought you might forget me if I was runner. It's awful tasting stuff, sister, no bon, no bon,' – 'no foloomin' bon' is his superlative phrase which he applies catholically to a cabinet minister of supposed ineptitude, a medical officer sparing of Blighty tickets, a non-picture hand at whist, or a suet pudding.

'Ah! that's the stuff to give 'em, sister. Come on, sergeant,' he invites, handing over some acid tonic and breaking into a minor key:

'*If the sergeant drinks your rum,*
  Never mind, nev-er mind,
If the sergeant drinks your rum,
  Nev-ver mind,
  He's entitled to a tot,
  But not the bally lot,
(Still) *If the sergeant drinks your rum,*
    Never mind,
      Nev-ver mi-ind.'

'Oh, stow yer 'ymn o' 'ate,' urges the sergeant.

'Shall I give you a hand till the orderly comes, sister? I'm very handy at bed-making really. As a matter of fact I'm quite an all-round handy person – make a good wife for somebody. Now, laddie,' as we tug up the mattress, 'up you go…and the best of luck,' for he cannot refrain from finishing the tag. 'Mercy, kamerad,' he suggests as the patient lifts his arms out of the way of the bedclothes. Then, as his head goes rather near the chart board, 'Haud yer 'eed doon, monn,' another tag which he hurls at people dipping under the eaves of the tent, or under the tunnel between the marquees or into the annexe – and which one day he explained.

'You know, sister, we were once in the trenches

with some Jocks on our left, and all day long it was, "Haud yer 'eed doon, monn, the's a sneeper aboot,"' – a phrase which must be spoken aloud rather quickly, and in broad Scotch to be thoroughly appreciated.

'Nahpoo,' he sadly overworks all day long. 'Nahpoo,' he says gazing on his hand at nap. 'Nahpoo the possy,' he comments, peeping into the jam tin. 'Nah-poo the bergoo,' he remarks as he disposes of the last spoonful of breakfast porridge. 'Nahpoo the Allemang, nahpoo the bully beef,' he cheerfully and confidently sings as he plays with his picture puzzle. 'Gam, stow it,' he would have said at one time to the teller of a tall story. 'Nahpoo,' he now growls scornfully and disgustedly, and in moments of additional stress 'Nahpoo, fini.'

'I believe there's a war on' and 'before peace is declared,' are two of his pet phrases. 'I believe there's a war on, sister,' he hazards, on first sipping the tea made to hospital standards, and not to his mother's 60-horse-power, brewed strong enough to 'make the spoon stand upright.'

'For the duration' is another favourite phrase. If m'mslle at the estaminet were tardy, he would certainly ask her if she thought he were there 'for the duration.' If his partner at draughts took what he considered to be too long in thinking out the next move, he would inform the assembly that they were presumably both there 'for the duration.'

'I clicked for beds and sister's told me off now,' I hear him informing the orderly. 'I'll cut the bread if you like. I seem to be the onion this afternoon.'

'You the onion!' laughs the orderly. 'I like that, don't come it over me with that yarn. It's gassed, sonny, gassed. It's tanked.'

'Um, but you won't say that when I've cut up umteen loaves, eh?'

'Oh! carry on. It will keep you out of mischief. So double up to it.'

'That's a dud,' he remarks, when he finds the first tin of butter empty. Then 'where are these tins dumped?' He never by any chance throws anything away. He always 'dumps' it.

Finally he seats himself and brandishes a knife gaily.

'What did you do in the Great War, daddy? Dodged Fritz & Co., my boy, slunk about hospital, swinging the lead, cutting up the rooty, ladelling out the stingo, handing out the possy and the doolay. Isn't that a record for an old sweat? Aah, I'm afraid I'm a wash-out, a sinful old perisher. What do you say, rookie?' addressing a young recruit. 'You want a backsheecoat?

Hello! I didn't know you were in the Labour Battalion? Ten-shun, slope wheelbarrows.'

'What is sister doing?' as I stumble over the mat. 'Oh, sister, you're not trying to work your tickets, are you?' 'Working England tickets' consists of 'scrimshanking,' malingering, or courting disaster purposely.

'Don't you think I'm useful, sister? I think *après la guerre* those in this ward ought to run a boarding house. I could be kitchen maid and waiter, "Lightning" could dust and sweep, the orderly could do all the rough work – special emphasis on the "work," and loud pedal on the "rough" – and Rookie could be the messenger boy.'

'And I'd make the beds.'

'Oh, no, sister, you'd be the lady with the frizzed hair that takes the money.'

I make assurance that I am overwhelmed by such a symbol of trust as the guardianship of the money, and I laughingly betake myself into the next ward where some work awaits me.

I hear him pattering round 'handing out the rooty and the possy, the stingo and the doolay,' and promising some one *a nissue* – otherwise a ration cigarette. Then when everything is ready I hear him subside into a deck chair, where I can imagine him at his ease remarking, 'Now, boys, let's get on with the war,' or 'Nah, then, wot abaht it?'

Chapter XVII
Some of my Boys

H<small>E WAS A</small> Greek god with a baritone voice and he came 'fra' Oadam,' more usually known as Oldham. He knew more parodies of songs than I had ever known existed, and all day long except at meal times we had such ditties as 'My little grey home in the Trench.' 'A little bit Jack Johnson fell from out the sky one day,' and 'Nahpoo the Allemang, nahpoo the Bully Beef,' the latter being, I think, scarcely a drawing-room song, for I have never been able to persuade any one to sing it me in its entirety.

He had a slight muscular trouble in his left shoulder, and was sent to us for a few days from a casualty clearing station *en route* for a rest camp, and to revert to his base. Of course he was up and about all day, and his great feat was carrying round for me the medicine basket to each tent, and standing by as I administered each dose.

Needless to say, remarks trickled forth subconsciously. 'Now, draftie, down with the drink.' 'A drop of port for you, sonny,' as I poured out the ferri and amm. cit. 'Wake up, me lad, here's your rum ration. Look how he springs to attention at the mention of "rum," sister. One of your tender years ought to sign the pledge. Give this one an extra dose, sister, to get even with him. He's a policeman in civvy life. Ugh' – reading his diet sheet – 'chicken, beef tea, eggs, jelly. Isn't this a policeman's holiday?'

'Kelly, sister? What! the one from the Isle of Man? Here he is, and next to him there's Douglas. Upon my word, now, isn't that a cute arrangement? A mustard plaster, sister,' – handing me the tin and breaking into melodramatic accents and a verse of 'Little Jim,' – 'I feel no pain, dear mother, now. Are we down-hearted? No, but he jolly soon will be when that plaster begins to bite.'

'A wee doech and doris,' as I pour out some sodii sal. 'Hoch, hoots, mon Jock. Ah cood fair greet tae see sae bonny a drap feending sae feckless a haame. Ferri. phos., sister, is that to give this man an appetite? Why, he could eat anything, he could eat a flock bed.

'Sorry, sister, I'm afraid I talk too much,' looking at me and hoping for a disclaimer. 'Do I?'

'Old Dads,' as the men called him, was a member of the 'Greybeards' Battalion,' and when in the forest cutting trees for trench supports he had injured his hand – an accident which brought him to my acquaintance.

At first the sisters' presence in the wards embarrassed his sense of the fitness of things, and our social rank seemed somewhat of a puzzle to him. On occasion he put finger to forelock, and addressed us as 'Mum,' 'Ma'am' and 'Me lady,' at other times it was 'Yes, sir' and at others 'Miss' in tones reminiscent of a customer to a waitress at a cheap restaurant. Finally he managed with great difficulty to learn the usual form of address.

He was infinitely grateful for what we did for him, and had a habit of talking under his breath while we did his dressing which was both amusing and disconcerting.

'You are good ter me. God knows you are. You are kind ter me. The Lord knows you are. I'm better looked after here than I've ever been in my life. I'm sure I am. I never knew there was so much kindness in the world. I'm sure I didn't. You 'ave ter work 'ard.

I'm sure you 'ave. I wouldn't like a daughter of mine to after do it.'

Whether he considered the work beneath the dignity of his daughter or whether he wished to spare her its excesses, I was never quite sure. More probably the latter, for he was a thoughtful and kind old man.

The last I saw of him was as he was being carried out on a stretcher to proceed to England – a recumbent figure swathed like a Polar explorer in great coat and scarves and a Balaclava, and still he was muttering – 'They have been good ter me. I'm sure they have. They were kind ter me. The Lord knows they were.'

'Sonny' was not quite seventeen years old, military age nineteen. He was a tall slip of a youth with a nature as bright as a June day, and eyes as blue as its skies. He came into hospital with tonsilitis, and he was up and about in a day or two, following me round like a little dog.

'Sister, can't I carry that for you? Sister, mayn't I cut those lemons? Sister, I'm a good sewer. Can't I stitch that curtain? Let me thread your needles.'

He told me much of his home affairs, and also of his disgust at getting so near to things, and yet not being sent into the trenches.

'You see, sister, people at home will say I'm a coward if I don't go up the line. I want to go up after a V.C., I haven't any one special at home to think about. I have no father or mother, only a sister and she's married. Her husband is one of the best, but they have two kiddies, and I'm not necessary to them or to any one, so it wouldn't matter if I went West. It's chaps like me that can be spared. We're the sort that ought to get knocked out.

'My sister sends me a parcel every fortnight, and she always sends my favourite supper-dish, a tin of pineapple and a tin of condensed milk. Have you tried it, sister? It's luscious, tray bon, trez beans. Do have it for your supper, sister. You would like it.'

Repartee and jokes were his forte.

'What are *you* doing in a regiment like the Buffs?' some older patient asked him.

'The Buffs, my boy?' Sonny retorted. 'Because they are the Best Unit For Foreign Service. See?'

One day he came to me and inquired, 'Are you fond of music, sister?'

'Why, of course,' I replied.

'Then here's a whole band for you, sister,' volunteered the young scapegrace, holding out the small rubber band from the mouth of a soda-water-bottle.

I laughed as I went on with my work. 'Quite right of you not to accept, sister. It's not worthy of you,' moving it round in his fingers, and disclosing the fact that it was split across. 'It's only a broken melody.'

'Pewcy' the other boys called him, though that was not the N. or M. given to him in his baptism. 'A regular entertainment he is,' said a Kiplingesque soldier, 'a fair Daisy,' – a criticism begot by the fact that Pewcy talked in italics. He used the latest slang, he brushed his hair an alarming number of times a day. He used to say 'Excuse me,' 'Allow me,' 'Will you please?' and 'Do you mind?' In a word, Pewcy was genteel, and gentility is the one thing at a discount on the Western Front.

The other men laughed at and made a great butt of him, and one of them used to imitate how Pewcy would say in the trenches, 'There's a beastly Boche, haw. What shall I do, haw? Shall I kill him or shall I smack his beastly face, haw?'

Poor Pewcy! When the July push came his regiment 'went over,' and he was one who proved himself a soldier and a man.

'Canada' had been blanket bathed, and duly installed in bed before I had had time to give him more than the briefest attention. Then, however, I went to see if he was warm and comfortable.

'Comfortable, sister,' with a blissful sigh of contentment. 'I've never slept between sheets for four years,' a circumstance which I asked him to explain.

He had been in Canada three years before war broke out, had 'had it pretty rough,' had been fur-trapping three hundred and ninety miles north of the Hudson Bay. On the outbreak of war he had come south, and joined the army without having a night in an hotel, so one could quite understand how he and sheets had been strangers for so long.

He came at a time when we were having a short-lived lull, and I had time to listen and to beguile him to talk of his trails, his shacks, the habits of the bear, the wolf, the lynx and the sable. He used to tell me of a snow-clad earth, a racing dog sleigh, the cold pinge of an atmosphere fifty or sixty degrees below zero, until I imagined it was a book of Jack London's to which I was listening.

Then, unfortunately, the lull came to an end. Convoys were arriving, beds were wanted, 'Canada' would take longer to get well than A.S. conditions can deal with, so he was regretfully evacuated to England.

*

He came from the Midlands, and described every one as a 'card.' Certainly he himself was a 'card.' He was transferred to the surgical hut from a marquee via the operating theatre and was placed on the bed, a limp figure reeking of chloroform. A few minutes later he had shot up in bed, and astounded us all by demanding in a loud voice, 'Who's swinging the lead?' this evidently prompted by the remark of a passing orderly.

'Here, lie down, colonel,' said this same orderly, helping to suit the action to the word with considerable dispatch, for the patient had a head wound.

'I'm not a colonel, I'm a full-blown private.'

'All right. Lie down, full-blown private.'

Quietude for a while as he gazed round. Then, – for he had been transferred to a ward where we had all the head cases – 'I'm in the wrong dug-out. Who brought me here? I want to go to the other dug-out for my tabs. I left two hundred tabs there. Can't I go, sister?'

His memory for a few days was rather uncertain, and one of his idiosyncrasies was to affirm that he had had nothing to eat. One afternoon he was telling me he was 'starved,' and I said 'Oh, come, now, surely not. Tell me what you have had to-day.'

'Well, I've had my temperature and my pulse, some

medicine and a pill, a bath and my bed made, and a needle in my arm. But that's all.'

I admitted that it certainly wasn't a very satisfying diet, but since I had personally fed him at dinner time with a large plateful of minced chicken, mashed potatoes, and bread, followed by two plentiful helpings of delicious custard pudding, I really did not feel unduly anxious about any dietetic deficiencies.

After a few days he got along in truly marvellous fashion, and to our inquiries was always 'A.1 at Lloyds, sister,' 'Splendid, I'm only swinging it now. I'll be able to put off my turban' – his head bandages – 'indoors very shortly, shan't I, sister?' He 'chipped' the other men ceaselessly, and soon was in such good form that, to our loss and his delight, he was whisked off to Blighty.

There are lots and lots of other boys, too, whom it is a pleasure to remember.

'Ike' – he had somewhat of an out-size in noses – was a delightful man, just a common every-day sort of Tommy, with no 'birth,' little education, and, on the surface, nothing particularly attractive about him. Yet there was something extremely likeable in his nature. I suppose it was 'jest his way.'

There was a boy, too, who hailed from 'Noo Yark,' and who guessed he wasna goinga stay outa precious scrap like this, especially if he could help a Britisher and do down a durned German. The dressing tray he alluded to as 'this dope,' and the Medical Officer as 'the quack.' He used to talk of handing people the lemon, and one night when he had toothache, he expatiated on the virtues of a dandy dentist of his down Pittsburg way. A man he suspected of swinging the lead he referred to as a great husky guy, and the Blighty cases he spoke of as the men who were recommended for shipment to England.

'Call 'em live freight and be done with it, Yank,' the other boys suggested.

There was an acute gastritis boy, too, one who was so ill he could not take the bananas I was handing round to all the other patients, so as I passed his bed I dropped a half-blown rose on his pillow.

'Oh, sister, it reminds me of home and my garden,' and he picked it up and kissed it – a pathetic little action I pretended not to see.

Then again there was 'Chikko' – as the men dubbed him – aged seventeen, who laughed his way through life, and who refused to cure himself of the excellent habit even if there was a silly old war going on. 'Wings' was in the 'Royal Flying Corpse, sister. I hope you'll always keep a bed ready for me here, as I'm sure to drop in one night, accent on the "drop." Possibly I'll come through the roof of the sisters' mess, and won't there be a mess! Pardon, sister.'

Excellent boys all of them. It has been an education and a pleasure to know them, and to work among them.

Chapter XVIII
Active Service in the Rain

THE MORNING DAWNED bright and warm, so warm that the up-patients took out their chairs and sat on the grass which does duty as lawn, while the tent walls were rolled back for the benefit and pleasure of the bed patients.

The sun was so ingratiating that it wooed one or two boys into doing 'a bit o' weeding' in our 'garden,' and into transplanting some horticultural specimens, so anaemic and so badly suffering from debility that their genus could not be determined. 'And good transplanting weather, too,' prophesied the rheumatic patients. 'We shall have rain before the day is out.'

About noon the rain comes, sending us all on duty after lunch, fully armed against its torrential attentions – two pairs of stockings, gum boots, shortest dress, belted mackintosh, together with sou'wester in place of, or over, our cap, since diving in and out of dripping tents soon gives one's stiffest, starchiest cap the appearance of a time-worn dish rag, added to which is the obvious danger of achieving a portentous cold.

One goes on the rounds with a medicine basket filled with half-a-dozen bottles, a couple of medicine glasses, towel, and small rinsing bowl. No sooner does one leave the tent than a particularly spiteful gust of wind comes, raises one's mackintosh like a balloon, and flaps the towel – which has hitherto been folded, but is now rebellious – with stinging lashes on one's hand, the rain pinging on one's face with seemingly delightful venom.

One struggles along and nearly tumbles into each tent, the wind is so typically March. Then another round is made with mouthwashes, gargles, and inhalations, the while one gets nicely soaked dipping under the tent eaves, and has rivulets running off one's sou'wester and down one's back. Next follows the round for straightening, and possibly remaking beds, with the consequent stripping of the mackintosh and, perhaps, sou'wester in each tent. Meantime the rain has gained in vigour and persistence, so much so, that it finds out the faulty parts in the tent roof and walls.

The orderly is called, and together we go round seeing to the closing of those ventilators which are allowing the rain to enter, placing bowls to catch innocuous drippings, pulling forward beds out of harm's – and the rain's – way.

Teatime comes, and so does the ward sergeant with 'warnings' for the England cases – 'a quarter-of-an-hour, sister.' One hurries from tent to tent, completes the filling-in of Blighty tickets, sees that the quite naturally excited travellers have had a plentiful tea, and that their kit is quite correct, hurries to the duty tent for a better scarf than the one with which a departing hero is contenting his happy self, bids goodbye all round, and splashes back to a tent, where an orderly has just reported four new admissions.

Temperatures are taken, blanket baths set in progress. Then one wades back to the nursing quarters through a paddock pied with rain-spattered daisies, dripping cowslips, and celandine. A gust of wind and rain considerably assist one's entry into the hut containing our bunks.

One throws off sou'wester and mackintosh, draws off gum boots, and attempts to remove, at least, a small portion of the thick clayey mud with which they are richly encrusted. Then comes a change of stockings and dress, leaving the other woefully bedraggled skirt spread out to dry over one's camp bath, and enviously commending the forethought of the wise virgin who has had an over-skirt made from a ground sheet. Then off to the mess room for a much appreciated cup of tea before going back to duty.

Here trouble meets us at the outset, for a particularly energetic gust of wind has blown down the duty tent, and we find an orderly and a medical officer crawling under the flapping tarpaulin preparatory to righting matters. The pole is soon hoisted, and while great execution is being done with a tent mallet, every human being in sight begins chasing after the diet-sheets, temperature charts, Blighty tickets, and laboratory slips which, presumably glad to escape from the privacy of the duty tent, are rioting giddily overhead. A tantalising chase it is, for many of the papers settle just long enough for us to almost reach them before whirling waywardly up, and successfully out of reach again.

A return to the duty tent shows us, oh! what a fall was there. We look round, and 'I would that my tongue could utter the thoughts that arise in me.' Inhalers and measures have been broken, medicine bottles overturned and smashed, the medicine cupboard has suffered in the encounter and has disgorged

THE ORDERLY OFFICER TO THE RESCUE

'The orderly officer to the rescue.'
— from Bob Cherry

much of its crowded contents, so that on the floor in an unsavoury-looking stream of tincture of iodine, tine. benz. co., methyl sal., and mist, alba., are to be found one-grain tablets of calomel, No. 9 pills, No. 13 pills, A.P.C. powders, soda bicarb. tablets, and similar little delicacies.

A comparative degree of order being restored in a superlative degree of haste, the marquees are once more visited. Ground sheets are pulled across the doors of the tent, the lights are lighted, gramophones tinkle. Darkness has come, the planks laid between the tents to serve as footpaths become sodden, and hurrying feet occasionally skid and sideslip on them.

Once something furry scuttles by within an inch of one's toe, and one has visual example of the familiar expression, 'a half-drowned rat.' Another round of the tents with gargles, inhalations, and medicines, and then an hour's work with beds. This up-patient has not noticed that the rain has been falling on his pillow. The position of his bed is altered, and a new pillow obtained. Drippings have been falling on the overturned portion of sheet on another bed, so that must be remade in part, and a clean, dry sheet substituted. Another bed has had its counterpane slightly splashed, but a folded towel inserted between it and the blanket meets every possibility of danger.

And so on we go until we are assured that every patient is warm, dry, and comfortable, and likely to remain so.

'A dirty night for you, sister,' the boys remark as we scramble into trench-coat and sou'wester.

But we have grown quite philosophical and stoical about the weather, besides isn't rain good for the complexion? And one day, I suppose, we shall remember we once possessed a complexion and will want to regain it, – in those far-off coming days *après la guerre*.

Chapter XIX
Sounds of Hospital Life

O F COURSE IT would be *comme il faut* and according to tradition to say that the sound that reached one's waking ears was the crowing of the cock, but, primarily, I am a truth-at-any-price person, and, secondarily – no, primarily, again – I am of the dormouse variety.

Thus, it takes a heavily footed batman with big army boots to parade the hut several times and splash relays of water into several waiting jugs before my sleepy ears are assaulted. Then, indeed, I do hear the cock crow, for in the nursing quarters we possess two spoiled darlings of bantams, Christopher and Emma, and Christopher is very vociferous, very lusty in the lung.

A hurried douche and dressing, with sundry

154

scufflings in adjacent bunks, reminding one of the sound of so many horses tossing in loose boxes, then comes the mess bell. Breakfast and then another bell, for our staff is so large that a later breakfast had to be instituted for 'two-stripers,' a concessionary half-hour which has led sleepy V.A.D.s to wish they had had the perspicacity to make a profession of nursing.

In the wards in the early morning one loses the sense of sound of outside things, but when temperatures are taken, medicines given, beds made and tent walls rolled back, one becomes conscious of 'Lef…wheel,' 'Eye…srite,' 'Form foss,' and the dull thud of marching feet.

Bang, bang…snap, snap, snap…spit, spit, from up the Bull-ring way, continues so evenly one loses the realisation of it. The medical officer, gargles, inhalations, foments and special medicines close one's ears until the clatter of crockery warns one for 'Come to the cook-house door, boys. Come to the cook-house door.' We hurry to cut thin bread, and butter for a patient who would like 'something to help down the milk,' to get toast snippets for another to coax down some beef-tea, and to see that certain special diets are duly administered.

In the afternoon 'another letter from Martha, another letter from home,' urges one or two boy-blues to put on their long overcoats – invariably to be greeted with 'Chelsea pensioner' – and go for the mail. 'Let's get out the gramophone and have a tune,' suggests one of the boys.

What a boon gramophones are! – as great a boon as that of card games. We are eternally grateful to the French king for whose benefit the card game was originated, and we equally bless the inventor of the gramophone.

Our gramophones suffer from the common complaint of most people and things on active service – they are sadly overworked. So much so that after a few very crowded hours of glorious fame they grow capricious, wilful, and finally stubborn.

But the boys are capable of marvellous achievements in the way of repairs. Once the spring of the gramophone broke – I need scarcely use the word 'once,' for this is a most frequent accident. On this particular occasion, however, I was rather distressed about the occurrence, for the gramophone was borrowed, and to acquire another spring takes much persuasion, a wait of three or four weeks, and, incidentally, twenty or so francs. The boys assured me it would probably be very easily mended, and I left the matter so.

Returning later to the marquee, I was horrified. A couple of newspapers were spread over the table, and, apparently, a kind of engineer's bench was strewn all over the papers.

Every screw in the gramophone which would unscrew was unscrewed. Every pin that would come away had come away. Every fitted part that would undo was undone. Practically every patient had his finger – or, worse still, his ten fingers – in the *mélange,* while the two bed patients at either side of the table were tendering much unwanted and disregarded advice, and soiling the sheets by their examination of loose nuts.

Then, cook-house bugle sounded, and they gathered up the scattered fragments and wrapped them in the newspapers.

Tea presumably refreshed and strengthened them from the fray, for after tea they got the spring from its easing and put it in the fire. Then they brought it out and hit it with a tent mallet, and the spring recoiled and hit one of them. They broke a pair of scissors and a jack-knife, bent a tin-opener and a bed-key, utilised the end of a milk tin, some string, and a bent safety-pin – *but* they mended the gramophone.

The men quite often whistle and hum to the tune of the gramophone, and sometimes they sing and harmonise so sweetly. Once they did so to the music of – a mouth-organ! Now I had always been trained to a great aloofness and something of an intolerance with respect to the mouth-organ. But, it seems, there are mouth-organs *and* mouth-organs. This one was evidently of the *and* variety.

For a time I was amused at the rapt expression, the absorbed air, and twisted features of the player, as with head so much on one side as to be almost parallel with his shoulder he passionately exhorted the instrument to sound.

Then from one tune to another, he drifted into 'Home, Sweet Home.' One boy began to whistle very softly. Then another, and another, until all joined in verse and refrain, verse and refrain.

I was quietly rubbing a patient, and not an alien sound was to be heard in the ward. The last note died away, melancholy and lingering, and for quite a minute no sound was made.

Then we all looked at one another, some one laughed, and we all joined. There are occasions in life when it is wise to laugh.

Chapter XX
More From My Diary

TOMMY IS A sentimental cuss. A certain nurse took a bunch of forget-me-nots down to the ward yesterday morning, and last night, in rather mystified tones, remarked that it seemed very depleted. A huge grin from one end of the marquee to the other! Then confession.

Practically every man had taken a spray of forget-me-nots to enclose in a letter to his 'girl.' Some of the little flowers had gone to Australia, some to California, some to Winnipeg, some to South Africa, and some to the British Isles – and some of the 'girls' had been married twenty years!

Yes, Tommy is a sentimental cuss, and surely we nurses are worse. For didn't that selfsame sister make a special visit to the market to buy another relay of forget-me-nots for the boys in the other tents!

Quite an exciting time this afternoon. Another nurse and I were washing our hands in the duty tent, when we heard the fire alarm, and looking out saw the wall and roof of a marquee in adjacent lines on fire. We cleared the tent ropes at a bound, and raced off calling to the orderlies to bring fire extinguishers and fire buckets.

Several men were already throwing on water and using extinguishers, and we two helped the sisters get the patients out of that tent and one very near to it. It was rather weird hearing the crackling and sizzling overhead as we worked.

As ill-luck would have it, the cases were all surgical, several with back, chest, and lower limb injuries. Those who could hobble were taken out wrapped in a blanket, the others were carried out in bed, and I don't remember one of them feeling heavy.

The orderlies soon had the fire under, and no one was any the worse except for a drenched tunic or a bedraggled cap. What lent celerity to our actions was the knowledge that a marquee can burn down in three or four minutes.

When I returned to duty, a new tent roof and sides had been put up, the ward cleaned, and no trace left of the fire. Quick work.

To-day I went into a ward expecting to find some freshly-made tea for one of my sick boys. Instead, I found the tea boiling industriously on top of a red hot stove after having been brewed a quarter-of-an-hour.

'It's my fault, sister,' volunteered one boy. 'I told them it was time to make it, but I have since discovered my watch was ten minutes fast,' holding out a very active-service watch with cracked glass, and quite an accumulation of dirt on the dial. 'If my watch wasn't in such a delicate state,' continued the unabashed culprit, 'I'd knock its wretched face off for being so fast and forward.'

The Australian sisters asked the remainder of our nursing staff to coffee last night, it being Anzac night. Some bright individual suggested our dressing for the event in fancy dress, and we all took up the idea with gusto. Why? Because, having to work hard, we like to play hard, too, – and we so rarely get the latter opportunity. Besides, most people, especially when they occur in numbers, rarely outlive the childish love of 'dressing up.'

So some of the girls put on their kimonos and came as Japanese ladies, and one put on her mackintosh, sou'wester and puttees, and called herself a back-to-the-land young Amazon. Another draped her 'wardrobe' curtain of spriggled muslin around her in pannier fashion, wore a white blouse, and tied a ribbon round her summer hat and came as a shepherdess. She looked delightfully pretty.

One found an overcoat and a concertina in the Red Cross stores, and came as an itinerant musician, and when we heard her samples of music, we were glad she was itinerant, and didn't mind how soon, nor how far, nor how long, the itinerary was.

Another came as a 'Blighty case' in khaki mackintosh, khaki scarf muffled to the ears, 'dinkum Aussy' hat, and feet and legs swathed in bandages and encased in immense trench slippers. She had the usual two 'Blighty tickets' appended, duly filled in, and with the information that 5,000,000 units A.T.S. (anti-toxin-serum) had been given!

One martyr had draped her brown army blanket around her, and done entangling feats with her hair and ruinous things with her complexion to represent herself as an Indian squaw. Others wore Australian hats, loose blouses and ties, and V.A.D. skirts as bush girls, thus paying compliment to our hostesses.

After songs and games, drinking coffee and nibbling sandwiches, we gave cheers for all Australian nurses and all Australian boys, for whom some of us have such a partiality that we are accused of having the familiar complaint of 'Australitis.'

And so to bed, as Pepys would say. The worst, however, of an Anzac night is that it is followed by an Anzac morning. As one girl said when the batman woke her at getting-up time, 'I thought to myself "Dear me, I hope I'm not going to have a bad night."'

As many as possible of the nursing staff were asked to attend the funeral this afternoon of a V.A.D.

When we arrived at the cemetery it was just in time to join the cortege.

A cordon of R.A.M.C. lined the road, and down it passed the padre followed by the pipers wailing a dirge. Next came the coffin, a plain, unstained wooden one covered with the Union Jack. Then came the A.D.M.S., and some other staff officers, and then we nurses – Q.A.I.M.N.S., Territorial, Reserve, St. J.A.A., and B.R.C.

We grouped ourselves round the grave, and the padre read the address exquisitely and most impressively. It was a beautiful spring afternoon with a fleckless blue sky and floods of soft sunshine. A bird on a bough swayed up and down up and down, with a continual cheep-cheep, cheep-cheep. We all stood taut and still, at attention, and the words rolled magnificently to us.

'Lord most holy, O God most mighty, O holy and merciful Saviour, thou most worthy Judge eternal, suffer us not, at our last hour, for any pains of death, to fall from Thee.'

The Union Jack is folded and laid aside, the pageantry and the impressive dignity of the scene loses its grip on one. Instead there comes to mind a picture of the dead girl, white and still, with closed eyes and crossed hands. We hear the rattle of ropes, the coffin is lowered, the swaying bird becomes a blurred vision. A French peasant woman with a tiny bunch of half-faded violets is sobbing loudly. The grave faces of the English nurses grow a little more set.

Then come the prayers, the Last Post – poignant and haunting – and the volley. Two French nurses drop into the grave a bunch of carnations, we take our flowers and lay them by the grave and turn to go back through the cemetery.

No matter what consolation is proffered, death is always an irreparable loss. But surely it is better to have it come when doing work that counts, work of national and racial weight, than to live on until old and unwanted.

And what a magnificent end to one's life, to lie there among those splendidly brave boys in the little strip of land which the French Government has given over in perpetuity to our dead. Thousands of the children that are to be, will come to such cemeteries, and will be hushed to reverence by the spirits of those who are not, by the spirits of the fallen that will for ever inhabit the scene.

May eternal rest be given to the poor shattered body and glory eternal to the ever lasting spirit!

Such a charming remark was made to me to-day. He was the shyest of patients, so gentle, quiet and retiring, and as I tucked him in – somewhat silently, perhaps, for I had given up hopes of wooing him to talk – he looked up at my St. John's Ambulance Brigade badge and said, 'Sister, I know now what S.J.A.B. means. It stands for, "She's just a brick."'

A most interesting morning – had a peep inside an

A EUSOL FOOT-BATH

Army Veterinary Camp. At that end of the camp where we entered was a huge, rectangular tank, about twelve feet high, and with an inclined approach at one end and a descent at the other. The tank was filled with medicated water, and horses suspected of skin diseases were driven up the ascent and into the tank, across which they were obliged to swim to the descent on the other side; and the remarkable thing is that the horses are rarely refractory.

Near by was a small pond, cement-lined and filled with medicated water. This was used as a foot-bath, and in it were tethered to a post some horses with foot injuries. After the foot-bath, each was to have a eusol dressing.

Several slight surgical cases were in a compound.

'We have good and bad patients just as you do,' we were told. 'This rascal persists in biting his bandage and disarranging the dressing. It will be guard-room for you, old chap, if you don't mend your ways.'

But the 'old chap' took shamelessly little heed of the warning, and hobbled away off to a coterie of disabled friends, one with a huge bandage round the neck as though he were suffering from a sore throat, another with a huge swab and plaster on his nose, two others with ankle injuries, and a fifth evidently nearing convalescence.

The more serious surgical cases were in stalls. Each had his medical chart giving the diagnosis and, occasionally, the temperature. The latter, of course, is more frequently charted and a more important matter in medical cases of, say, pneumonia or bronchitis. Several drainage tubes were to be seen in wounds, the treatment of which is very much on the same lines as the treatment of human wounds.

The dispensary had its usual store of lotions, drugs, and medicines – the latter two much in request from the numerous coughs, colds, and heart troubles which exposure and a harrowing life bring in their train.

Near by was a rectangular piece of ground, cemented, covered with straw and ground-sheets, and with a pile of blankets. This was used as an operating table, and to it were brought the cases for operation. Hind and fore legs were tethered, and the patient was pulled down, chloroformed, covered with a blanket, and the operation began.

In an adjacent paddock, forty or so convalescents were being exercised by grooms who kept them trotting in a circle, the laggards and 'lead-swingers' being called to attention in a very firm, sergeant-major sort of tone that seemed to be more effectual than the cracking of the never-applied whip.

All those who have sampled the famous Maconochie stew will relish the flavour of a Scotchman's little joke cracked to-day in one of the wards.

Said this Jock to a member of a certain Highland regiment, 'But ye' no Scoatch, are ye?'

'Well, my father was Scotch, my mother was Irish and I was born in Greece, so what would you call me?'

Puff – puff – pu-u-ff.

Jock removes his stubby pipe, glances sideways and snorts out, 'Maaconochee.'

'A bit of a tickler, that!' gurgled out one of the boys when he was subsequently told.

'Aye, jammy!' was the apt reply.

The hard frost continues. This afternoon I was walking down the road when a convoy went out. The dust cloud raised by the cars from the dry, hard road was equal to that on a hot August day.

What a picture the cars made! All along the straight, tree-bordered road as far as the eye could see, was car after car, a long steady uninterrupted line of them, with no horse vehicle, and no pedestrians to break their uniformity. On and on they come in apparently never-ending succession, this car from a fleet of the White Rabbit, that from the Scottish Mobile Unit, that bearing the name of the 'Laird of So-and-so,' this 'The Minnies,' that 'The Maudes,' this an A.S.C. wagon from the Red Hand fleet, that from the fleet of the Black Star, this the gift of the Licensed Traders, that from the Scottish Textile Workers. The Red Cross ambulance cars go to prove we are a united nation.

Had a case of typhoid in one of the wards, so several boys in that particular marquee are to be inoculated. One boy informed me that he didn't think it would be necessary in his case as it was only six months since he had been tattooed, and tattooing was as good as inoculation, wasn't it?

Quite a number of the boys hold this belief. This particular one rolled back his sleeve, and showed me a red heart shot through with a large, blue arrow the size of a respectable lead pencil. Underneath were written the words 'Maggie, I love you.'

Such an unblushing parade of affection persuaded another man to show his arms, the one bearing the name 'Elsie,' and the other 'Agnes,' a situation which the other boys thought liable to be fraught with considerable danger. The possibility, however, of rivalry and jealousy was removed, when the man explained that they were the names of his two little daughters.

A woman's head in a befeathered hat, and a girl's name, are favoured subjects for tattooing, though the name, one fears, must place a terrible strain on the fidelity – or the veracity – of the gallant and impressionable martyr. A pantomime 'principal boy' is another favoured device. So, too, are clasped hands, while a man who has seen service in India quite usually boasts a coiled snake on the arm and a most elaborate blue and red dragon with out-stretched wings unfurled across the chest.

Even yet, I'm not sure whether the following piece of sarcasm heard to-day was intentional or not.

Two boys from the same town were talking of a home regiment.

'Who is the Medical Officer with the Loamshires now?'

'Captain Medico.'

'Medico! I went to school with him. You don't mean to say he's a doctor! '

'Yes, old son – and with the Loamshires.'

AN OPERATION AT AN ARMY VETERINARY CAMP

'Great Scot! He a doctor! Why, man, he couldn't hurt a fly! '

We had a thoroughly delightful and enthrallingly interesting lecture to-night when the radiographer explained to us X-rays and the working thereof, and showed us many plates of cases we had nursed. Wish all the lectures were as interesting.

To-day a guard was on duty in a 'shell-shock' ward where was a patient who persisted in wanting to get out of bed.

'Now be quiet, matey,' he exhorted. 'You must lie still, lie still, chum. No, you can't get up. Lie still, I say. If you don't lie still, I'll – I'll –,' the accents grew positively threatening – 'I'll bring the other guard.'

Chapter XXI
War-Time Marketing

'MA CHÉRIE, BE an angel and do some mess shopping for me this morning, since you are going into town,' pleads the home sister.

I hesitate, for off-time has been none too generous of late. We are short-staffed and one's scanty leisure at any time is always pretty fully booked. So I hesitate.

'It won't take long.' – I know it will take all the morning. – 'Besides, you know the business from A to Z,' continues the voice of the arch-flatterer. 'You will enjoy it. It is market day. There is an evacuation, and you'll get a good car to town. And you'll help me tremendously.'

When I leave the camp I don't take 'a good car.' It is a glorious, mild, springlike morning – a perfect morning, thoroughly to be enjoyed after a month's iron frost of twenty to thirty degrees, a morning when, if I were in mufti, I should feel shabby and go and buy a new hat, and then straightaway order a coat and skirt to correspond with it.

However, the Army, excellent institution that it is, decides our fashions, and on April 1st I shall don a new hat, a straw one, and not until April 1st. Moreover, it is a very dull pastime buying a new hat precisely like its predecessor, so my ebullition of up-liftedness and light-heartedness finds an outlet in another way. Instead of decorously taking 'a good car,' I am mounted on a great lumbering motor-lorry, the seat at least six feet above the ground. Here I drink in great draughts of refreshing, sweet, pure air.

The driver and I 'talk shop,' *his* shop, though ultimately it veers round to mine. After meeting cows, young bullocks, pigs, flocks of sheep, and several of the most antediluvian of country carts, – all quaint enough to form the subject of an exquisite picture, – we encounter a tiny band of Indians with their goats. At this we abandon the subject of self-starters for that of the management of traffic.

'Of course, traffic is not so well regulated here as it is in England. Still, we have surprisingly few accidents.

During Christmas week, however, I knocked down a man, an A.S.C. bloke.

'He was admitted into hospital and I went that night to see him. "You fool!" was his greeting. I agreed.

'"You fool! Here I am being tucked into a cushy bed several times a day by kind-hearted nurses, bless 'em! All we patients are happy as the day is long. Everybody is busy making something to decorate the ward. Look at all the holly and mistletoe the boys are going to hang up. There are going to be concerts and Christmas teas and sing-songs and game competitions, and you, you fool, knock me down – and *don't hurt me sufficiently* to keep me here. I'm to be discharged to-morrow."

'And the poor blighter turned his face to the tent wall.

'You notice, we've got some women-drivers, sister. They'll be all right for the lighter base work, at E—— and H——, near the coast, but the usual ambulance-car driving is not fit work for a woman, with its night-work, and out in all weathers.

'You know, too, what it was in July. We had to disinfect and spray our cars several times during the day and night – and our own clothes had to go to the fumigator. Our shirts we had to change more than once during duty. And another thing. As you know, we sometimes hadn't a man as a case but, at the end of the journey, a dead body.'

'True,' I remark, 'but not one of your arguments is strong enough to urge against women doing their obvious duty in this ambulance work. What about us nurses? We have night-work, we are out in all weathers in our camp hospitals. We had the vermin nuisance last July, and, indeed, always have it – in a milder form, of course. While as for your last argument…'

'Yes, sister, but you nurses – well, you are just you.'

Marvelling at the inconsistency of man, I bid him good-morning, and go towards the market, calling to mind the heated opposition we always have from the boys when we sometimes say what we often passionately feel, that we nurses would gladly and proudly go as far up the line as we could be useful, and that it is our duty to take the same risks of being killed, wounded, or maimed as they.

But chivalry, it seems, is not yet dead, and this subject remains the only one on which the boys contradict and oppose us.

What is the first item on my shopping list? Eggs. I go towards the poultry section set apart under the shade

177

of Ecole des Beaux Arts, and flanked on the further side by a beautiful Gothic archway.

I am offered '*beaucoup* eggs,' as the boys would say, great yellow ones, at thirty centimes each. Why do eggs look so much more tempting when their shells are yellow? Emboldened by the size of my order for eggs, the market woman presses me to buy chickens trussed and ready for the oven at seven, eight, or ten francs. But what interests me more than the prepared fowls are the live ones with legs tied together and put down in odd places, three cockerels, for example, in company with a pair of great wooden sabots thrust into a string bag, which lies in the wide sill of a mullioned window, whose tiny, diamond-shaped panes are throwing back a myriad shafts of lights from the soft, February sunshine.

I pass a booth laden with aluminium rings *faites dans lestranchées*, and ornamented with tiny badges, small designs beaten out of spent cartridges and numerous chasings. Next to it is a stall for those post-cards which the boys adore, celluloid masterpieces emblazoned with polychromatic badges and flags, and decorated with a chaste salutation 'Forget-me-not,' 'To memory dear,' 'A kiss from France,' 'Ever of thee I'm fondly dreaming,' and so on. It is not at all unusual for one boy to send as many as four or five of these post-cards with its burning message to different, trusting (let us suppose!) damsels in England.

One stall contains biscuits, over a hundred different kinds. Hardly a war-time scarcity, evidently. The numerous refreshment booths have pain d'épice, madeleines, croissants, rolls, different kinds of pastries and brioche. How good is the latter, piping hot, with fresh butter and honey, and to the accompaniment of tea, which the English have now taught the French to make really well.

The delicacies on the booth presumably are chiefly for the indulgence of the market shoppers, not the stallholders. For one notices several of the latter frugally dining on a glass of *vin rouge* made warm with a little hot water and sustaining with an accompaniment of a hunch of dry bread, – quite a different meal to that of the denizens of Covent Garden, with their plate of 'hot roast,' their fish and chips, or their pot of tea and bulky sandwiches.

But *l'heure s'avance* and I have only worked one item off my shopping list. Even so my loitering foot-steps are waylaid at a china stall, where I buy for half-a-franc each some charmingly quaint, dull-brown casseroles. Thereby do I take time by the forelock, for such an opportunity as this morning's may not present itself again before spring comes, and the forest near us is a carpet of flowers, so many of which I shall want to commandeer for our marquees.

Rounding a corner towards the vegetable stall I behold two English Tommies making purchases of fruit. The stallholder is a girl of twenty or so, and she is smiling up at them roguishly as she presses her wares – which I deeply suspect of being somewhat overpriced – upon one of them, with a 'Oh, aah, m'sieu, mais c'est bon.'

And Tommy, as he ruefully disburses from a tiny belt pocket, is saying, 'Garn, yer sorsy cat!'

Potatoes at thirty-five centimes the kilo, dessert apples at fifteen centimes, oranges at ten centimes – how much nicer they appear served from the large tub-baskets which remind one of Marseilles! – cabbages at twenty-five centimes, cauliflowers at sixty, conclude my purchase at the greengrocery stall, where I am served by a very small, exceedingly old-fashioned, young person of twelve or thereabouts. She is dressed in a large checked, red and black, bouncing dress, a small checked, blue and white, bouncing apron, a shoulder tippet of black wool crochetted in three tiers, each edged with a scalloped-shell pattern. She has an exceedingly tight, exceedingly thin pigtail, – the end slightly swollen with a tightly bound barricade of white sewing cotton, – a very quick, disarming smile, and a very quickly upturned nose.

We exchange a wide, friendly smile, hers fading as she turns to seek a new customer, mine fading at Maman's leisure and typically French disinclination to make out *le facteur*.

Finally, she sweeps aside some swedes and carrots and makes a salient on the stall, where she rests her book of bills and aggrievedly writes out my account in thin, spidery characters. Then she takes out a red cardboard *porte billet*, bulging with the greasiest of one, two, five, and twenty franc notes efficiently held in place by a piece of the greasiest string, gives me my change, and we part amid elaborate courtesies.

A scrubbing-brush and some beeswax, – I create much merriment by my confession that I don't know what to ask for, but my need is *cire des abeilles*, which is immediately understood and translated as *encaustique,* – complete my purchases, and with the ordering of coal and coke my responsibilities cease.

As I write out the *laissez-passer* to admit the coal and the coalheaver into the camp, I inquire the price. 'One hundred and sixty francs the thousand kilo.'

Six pounds for nine and a half cwt.! What a price! As I leave the office, I conclude that the only comment which meets the situation is the old tag the boys adopt when other words seem superfluous: 'Sister, I believe there's a war on.'

Chapter XXII
History Makers

How many preconceived notions has the war swept aside! And among others of assuredly more weight is the school-days idea of a history maker. Every one who has dangled a satchel has had his, or her, idea of the men who made history, to the total exclusion of the great statesmen and the inclusion only of mail-clad heroes dashingly riding with fluttering pennons and picturesque accoutrements to the Crusades, of Henry V's swift-armed bowmen naked to the waist and with bare foot planted in the ploughed soil of Agincourt, of sturdy Ironsides, close-cropped and shovel-hatted, marching into action lustily singing their Psalms, of the dashing, scarlet-coated body of men who added to England's fame the unforgettable record at Balaclava – how they have fired our blood, and stirred our imagination! How we have thrilled and exalted over their doings!

And here we are living in the midst of history makers, men who have more than once taken part in deeds equalling and, on occasion, excelling that of Balaclava, and we readjust our notion of history makers, we correct our perspective, we humanise and individualise those makers of history. We realise that they were not men of superhuman nerve, muscle and endurance. We bring to mind for the first time the little, old-fashioned, girl-children, wimpled and with steeple head-dress waiting at home, the grey-robed Puritan wives a little sanctimonious and wholly anxious about those Cromwellian warriors, the Victorian wives, – big-hipped and tight-waisted, with smoothed hair in chenille hair-nets, – left to go through life without those fallen Crimean heroes. The men who made history were men. We are apt to forget that and think of them as so many lines and paragraphs of a history book.

And when the standard histories of this war come to be written, no doubt they will be done by terribly efficient old gentlemen who wear pince-nez and have taken high honours in Classical Tripos. They will be written probably in polysyllabic prose and in epic style. They will abound in references to policies and constitutions, to treaties and conventions, and probably posterity will be deluded, momentarily perhaps, into thinking of our history makers as imposing personages clothed in scarlet, ermine-bordered, or august figures endowed with the fearsome dignity of Mars.

But for my short span I shall refuse to forget that among the makers of history in our great age there were Tommy Brown and 'The Colonel,' and 'Aussy' and 'Papa.'

Tommy came to us in the big push of July 1916, military age twenty, real age eighteen. He had a gunshot wound in the head, was trephined, had a cerebral hernia, and for a time got along very nicely. He was great friends with another little boy whose bed we moved next to his – and 'the Heavenly Twins,' 'David and Jonathan,' and 'the Children,' were some of the names they received. The other little boy had a hernia and had been trephined; he had forgotten a great deal and was to teach such little things as the swallowing of a pill, the fastening of a button, the necessity for mastication, and so on.

During the day we used to put 'the Children's' beds in the sun, give them Japanese sunshades, drinks, fans, picture papers, and cigarettes, and quite a good time they used to have together. Every one in the camp knew them and used to exchange greetings and bring them little gifts, until at the end of the day's levee their lockers used to be well-stored pantries of chocolate, fruit, sweets and biscuits.

Then Tommy began to 'go back.' He commenced having fits and obsessions. He didn't want to play with 'the Colonel,' as the other boy was called. He was irritated with the latter when he persisted, as he did dozens of times in the day, in clacking his tongue in imitation of our scurrying feet. 'Sister, sister,' was his continual cry if we moved out of his sight. 'Don't leave me sister,' he implored one afternoon.

'No, I won't. I'm just going to the next bed,' – about two feet from his own. 'I'm not really leaving you. I want to feed the Colonel.'

'No, sister, don't. He doesn't want you as much as I do.'

'Oh! but he wants his tea. Come, sonny, be a man.'

'No, sister, I don't want to be a man. I only want you,' and he used to put out a hot, little hand and grab belt or apron or skirt, a hand that clung in the extraordinarily tenacious fashion that a sick person's hands can cling.

One day in one of his more lucid moments he told me what his obsession was. When up the line, his company were entering some trenches taken over from the enemy, and the dead body of a German with black face and protruding tongue and eyes had been the first sight that greeted him. The boy in front of Tommy had, on entering the trench, caught his foot on the body with the natural result. Poor Tommy could not rid himself of the memory, and when the fits recurred it was the dead German who always pursued him.

Poor little Tommy! He was the only child of his mother, and she was a widow. She used to write him every day, and, as the days wore on, he could not even be troubled to have us open and read the letters to him. He just lay with his fingers closed on the day's letter. Then one brilliant morning of fleckless turquoise sky and golden light, he died very quietly and very peacefully, just slept away.

Poor little mother in black, no more listening for his welcome footstep, no more washing and sewing for him, no more cooking his favourite dishes, – nothing but a numbing monotony, an aching emptiness in the coming years. I crossed his hands and prayed an unsaid prayer. He lay like a carven figure on a tomb in some mediaeval vault. Poor little history maker!

It was one fine August morning when I made his acquaintance. I was dipping under the eaves of the tent when the ward-corporal brought along a batch of wounded from a convoy, and heading the queue was a roguish-looking individual with copper-coloured curls crisping round a head like that of an Olympian competitor. A tin hat a few sizes too small, a broad smile, and fun-laden eyes of intense blue was the impression one got of him as one hurried on.

He came into the marquee, was fed, bathed, and, evidently thinking his self-imposed silence of sufficiently long duration, broke into a babble of talk which never ceased until three or four days later he was evacuated to Blighty.

'You know, sister, I'm too great a rogue to die unhung, so Fritz won't get me. He's winged me this time, but he won't get me. Oh no, it's nor-too-bad, but, say, sister, is it a Blighty? Dinkum? That's the goods.'

A Ballarat men interposed.

'Am I from Aussy? Betcher sweet life. Been there, sister? Oh! you don't know what a country's like yet. Gosh, it's God's own country. You're going *après la guerre?* You'll never come back. Some squatter will snap you up.'

One or two English Tommies grin sheepishly and look up tentatively, but 'Aussy' careers boldly on.

'How are we doing?' he speaks to another patient, wounded a few days previously, from his own division.

'Oh, same as ever,' – then his love of an audience overcoming his desire to give authentic news, – 'You know, the Bosches have got a gun whose shells burst three times, don't you? Fact. But we've got a gun whose recoil brings up the next day's rations.' Turning to me, 'It's an Australian invention, sister. The man who invented it has been invalided home and runs a boomerang farm in Victoria.'

'It sounds like an Australian invention,' I drily agree, and some quality of my voice makes the other patients laugh.

'Oh, come off it, Aussy,' says the Ballarat man. 'Don't try kidding sister. She can do a bit in that line. She'd kid you up country without a tent.'

'Dinkum,' says the Queenslander. 'She'd kid you up a tree and chop it down while you stood on the branches.'

'She'd kid you down a well and cut the rope after she played out the bucket,' joins in the West Australian.

'All this sounds remarkably unkind,' – a vigorous disclaimer. 'But it gives point to my belief that before going to Australia I must learn the language.'

'There you are, Digger. That's the way she hands it out to us, doesn't half put it across us sometimes.'

Soon the talk drifts, as it always does when two or three Australians are gathered together, to 'Gyppo,' and as I run backwards and forwards I hear tales of the bonza old chap who was the only fair dealer in Alex and who gave you a bonza feed of Al tucker for five piastre; of the old beggars who used to cry 'Gibbe backsheesh, Australian;' of the news vend or who glibly repeated words taught him by a mischievous Tommy, and came calling 'Verra good news, 100,000 Australians killed,' and of how 'we cleared him out and gosh, he never touched the ground, sister. Awful crowd, we Aussies, you know. We're a fighting unit, not soldiers.'

And like so many naughty schoolboys they derive considerable satisfaction from my agreement that they are indeed 'terrible boys.'

The last day Aussy was in the wards, we had among other admissions a little boy who, when I asked him his name, fumbled and plucked at his tunic pocket, grew red in the face, continued to fumble, and finally drew out his pay-book and showed me his name.

It was Maconochie.

But alas! though I received the information in an appreciated silence, I could only shield him for the time being. His chart came down from the office shortly afterwards, and his name stood revealed for all who ran to read.

'Aussy' was merciless.

He held a court of inquiry as to what was to be done with 'the enemy,' but the sentence – to be carried out the following morning at dawn – was too gory, too piecemeal, and too culinary to be recorded here. Meantime, 'Fray Bentos, you've left the best part of your head over here,' throwing him his cap. 'Rations, lend me your razor. I expect you'll have one, since you've got almost a moustache.'

'Mixed veg, will you have a backsheesh fag?' – throwing him a ration cigarette. 'Irish stew, sling the possy over 'eere,' putting out his hand for the jam.

Maconochie, however, had lived his short life in Eastern London, and after the first short-lived shyness had worn away, showed himself no mean match for 'Aussy.'

'I guess you're some kid,' remarked the latter, as

191

Maconochie spun an enamelled plate to the ridge of the marquee and caught it behind his back.

'I guess you're some goat,' flashed back 'Fray Bentos,' as he dived into an adjacent annexe.

But unfortunately for the merriment of our existence, the ward-corporal came round a few minutes afterwards and warned 'Aussy' for England.

'Good-bye, sister, I'm real sorry I'm going,' – so was I, – 'I'd like to give you a souvenir, my rising sun, which has come with me from Australia, been through the Peninsula picnic, and then through this strafe in La Belle France. Good-bye, sister, and may your little shadow never grow less.'

He clumped out of the ward, a 'dinkum Aussy' hat pulled over his copper-coloured curls, his two labels tied to his tunic, and a sling holding up his 'boxing-glove' of cotton-wool and bandage which swathed the remains of his left hand. He had endeared himself to all in the ward, and he left behind him a streak of brightness which still occasionally shines on me. Happy young rogue, most unorthodox of history makers!

'Papa' was in the Foresters. He came to us in the fall suffering from bronchitis. He was admitted somewhat early in the morning, and I only had time to see him installed before the medical officer did his round. Then the resulting catechism disclosed some slightly surprising facts.

'Have you had this trouble long?'

'Off and on for a matter of five and twenty years. In the spring of 1882 I had pleurisy and—'

1882! Good gracious, years before one was born! One looks amazed at the hoary old die-hard.

'How old are you?'

He tells his age.

'I think you have done your bit, what do you say, sister?' as the 'Blighty tickets' are handed over.

'Well, sir, I have been discharged once' – a fit of coughing – 'have my discharge papers here,' hunting in his treasure bag during another fit of coughing, 'but I joined up again. Once a soldier always a soldier, sir, and I'm worth plenty young ones yet. Those who can help, ought to. I couldn't stand aside and do nothing, sir.'

Good old history maker! Would that all the male and female slackers could see and hear you, could look at the wrinkled face, the scant, hoary hair, the toil-worn hands, and know of your brave attempt to help your country in her heavy hour of stress. The Old Country cannot be so effete when she turns out men like you. It is men of your breed that has won and will keep for England her proud fame, eminence, and power.

Doughty old history maker!

Chapter XXIII
Our Boy-Blue Mail

'NOTHING MUCH FOR YOU,' says a nurse, turning from the table where the mail is spread out. 'A letter from a patient, judging by the writing.'

'Oh, is that all?' one grouses, taking up the note.

Now that little grouse is very culpable, for there is scarcely a nurse but receives at one time or other some very charming letters from patients, letters she will be glad to con over in the coming years, perhaps when she is a lonely old woman, and the full, crowded days of the present have become dim memories.

Most of the letters from 'our boys' are lame, halting, little expressions of thanks, laboriously written from an inarticulate mind and with the find-you-well-as-this-leaves-me-at-present style which, one thought, had been ridiculed out of existence. They are written on the most marvellous assortment of scrap paper that one could wish to see; but, of course, *papier de luxe* is scarcely to be associated with a dug-out. Letters from England come to us written on 'real' note-paper.

> 'DEAR SISTER – Just these few lines to let you know that I arrived all right, but we had it very rough, and a lot of the boys was ill but we got over it all-right. I am in a very good hospital, but I wish your hospital was over here. 'From your loving patient,
>
> '———'

The adjective preceding 'patient' may be taken as a matter of form.

> 'DEAR SISTER – Just a few lines hoping this will find you in the best of health, and all the boys in D 4. In regards myself, we had a pleasant voyage, and then we was sent to X——. Well we were treated very nicely and it is a beautiful hospital with plenty of nice food. It is in a building, more swanky than yours but not so jolly, the sisters is very nice but they dont laugh as much as you do and dont cheer a chap up so much.

Well Sister, it is a long way from London'
(his native place) 'but we must be thankful
to be hear, and you might remember me to
Sister F—— and Sister H—— also all D2
and D5 and D4 boys. Hoping they all get
Blighty and thanking you for your kindness wishing you the best of health and roll
on the end of the war from your obedient
patient No – .

'Pte. Joshua,
'1st East Mudshires,
'No. 2 Hut General Hospital,
'X——'

It is very nice to have one's smiles appreciated, and
very good to know that the boys never realise how
much it costs sometimes to remain cheery.

'DEAR SISTER – Just a little note to let
you know I havent forgotten C lines and the
sisters in that little part of France, hoping
to find you all in the best of health as this
leaves me here at present. Since I wrote last
I have been in the Trenches again among
the frozen snow but I only lasted a week

and then I had to come out swinging the lead with trench feet and got sent down to hospital again but I never had the good for tune to get to C lines No——. Never mind better luck next time.

'We're for it again to-morrow so I shall have to look out for another Blighty complaint.

'Well I think this is all this time so I will have to close this from

'Yours sincerely,

'Australia.'

'DEAR SISTER – A few lines in answer to your ever welcome letter and was pleased to hear that things were going on well with you all and thank you very much for the parcel of chocolate that you were so kind to send. It arrived in good condition and at a good time too, for we were going in. Pleased to hear little M's arm got on all-right and he got his tickets. He was such a nice fellow.

'Did it take you very long with the spring cleaning I wish I had been there to

help you because I know you would have
a lot to do.

'I will now close wishing you the very
best of luck, from

'Yours sincerely,
'Australia.'

The above deathless epistle had been read, signed
and censored by 'Australia's' officer who, no doubt,
was highly edified by his desire to be back helping
with the spring cleaning.

'DEAR SISTER – Having regained the use
of my right arm I thought I would endeavour
to scribble you a few lines to thank you for
your kind attention and tender care while
I was sick in that little bit of France known
to the C lines boys as a corner of heaven.
Well I have much pleasure in letting you
see I am in England. When I left C lines I
went to the Convalescent Camp and then
back to the Fritzes and there I stopped one
with my name and number written on it.
I stopped it with my right arm which got
a compound fracture in the right humerus

199

in two places, and I am quite happy and contented with my suvenoir presented to me on the 1st of July. I got hit about 8-45 ak emma while making an advance from the first German line to the second, and fortunately was able to crawl into a nice, large, comfortable shell hole and lay there till dark and then successfully crawled back to my own little dug out reaching it by 1 ak emma. By 5.30 ak emma I was miles from the trenches lying in a cosy cot detailing my experiences to a very nice sister from Bolton. I was under the painful influence that I had lost the use of the arm altogether, but I was X-rayed twice and now my arm is so much better that I am able to under difficulties scribble you these few lines. I hope you will return this scrawl if you are unable to read it. We are doing famous here, have been here a week and have been to two garden parties and a lovely motor drive 65 miles. Well I think I have completed my little portion of self-concerning news and so will now inquire of you. I trust you are quite well and not overworked by endless convoys. I would very much like to know how Sister H—— and Sister B—— are should you have the opportunity to state the same when you answer this awfull piece of correspondance. Well, sister, I have had a little piece of luck when at one of the garden parties. I won a wist drive and made my winning number of tricks when diamonds were trumps on the second to the last table I played at. I got a beautifully marked cigarette case, also a box of 100 cigs. Well I am afraid I must close it has taken me nearly an hour to niggle this terrible piece of work into this state, so now dear Sister I will wish you further success, a jolly time, a hasty conclusion to the dreadful war so that you may return home, also trusting to hear from you as soon as convenient to you and I do hope you write, kindly remember me to the other sisters and except the very kindest regards yourself and allow me to remain

'Your faithful patient,

'——

'P.S. It's grand weather here in Blighty we have less than two hours ago given 3 cheers for Tommies and Sisters in France, it was at the conclusion of a small concert in our Hall and it's a wonder you didn't hear us, best of luck to you all.'

The malapropisms are easily translatable. 'Ak emma' originates in the signalling system. P, E, D, V, and several other letters sound so similar from a distance that they are made Pip, Emma, Don, Vic, and so on. Thus a.m. becomes ak emma, p.m. becomes pip emma, an observation post, O.P., becomes O pip, V.A.D. would be vic ak don, and so on. The guileless manner in which the boy takes it for granted that I shall be interested in the exact circumstance of his winning the 'wist drive' is typically naïve and unaffected and a good index of the friendliness which exists between the sisters and the boys.

'DEAR SISTER – Just a few lines to let you know I am very near my home. I am at G——. It is a very large hospital and I am sending you a few picture postcards to let you have an idea of the place. I only regret

I was unable to stay in your 'hotel' for a longer period, for altho I was only a lodger for a day and two nights, yet I had quite settled down and feel sure I should have been perfectly happy. Kindly remember me to the Captain. Both your kindness I shall never forget wherever I may be, I remain,

'One of your grateful patients,

'G—— E——'

G—— E—— was in many ways a very interesting man. He was aged about forty, looked about fifty, had the dignity and courtliness of a man of sixty, and the heart of a boy of eighteen. He had lived in Paris for about twenty years, spoke and wrote French better than his own language, had all the jargon and slang of Paris on the tip of his tongue, – yes, he kept it there – and had the most wonderful collection of photographs of poiluchums that surely exists in the British Army. The following letter was written by a Public School and Oxford man with the distinguished rank of lance-corporal, and the most charming disposition imaginable.

'DEAR MISS——— You see I did not have

the good fortune to get to London after all' – (London was his home) – 'This was supremely bad luck, – and of a sort that one could not possibly fight against. You see our hospital ship made intimate acquaintance with a German torpedo and we had to take to the boats with much celerity and dispatch, – a very painful process to me as I had to walk up two companion ladders and climb over taffrails etc. unaided and on my groggy leg, – and after a somewhat harassing time to board a Destroyer that turned up most opportunely, and thence to X—— many hours late.

'So all arrangements for our disposal had to be altered, and I landed up here. Strafe it! However no lives were lost and they towed the hospital ship into port, and last, but not least, I am told our Destroyer sunk the submarine. So all's well that ends well. Meanwhile I am quite comfortably fixed up here, my leg is getting well much quicker than it needs to!! and my people are coming to see me to-morrow. So I have really nothing at which to grumble.

'I want to thank you most awfully for the really good time you gave me in C 4. It is a long time since I have so enjoyed a few days. I never knew before how kind sisters are to the boys: you certainly taught me a lesson all of you.

'With very kind regards to yourself and all my other friends in the ward I am,

'Yours sincerely,

'———'

The following letter was written by a Canadian boy, the fur-trapper who had not slept between sheets for four years.

'DEAR SISTER – I must make an attempt – or is it attack? – to write to you. I'm afraid as usual it will prove a failure.

'Firstly, you can't imagine how sorry I was to leave your hospital. It was almost as bad as leaving home when I went to Canada. I was perfectly miserable all the way across and, finally, was horribly seedy but am improving a little now and have practically no pain.'

205

(Then follows a remark about sisters, which modesty forbids me reproduce.)

'Don't forget about the Jack London book. I should love to read it with you, and talk about it. It is very simple but the descriptions are extremely good. The first story is rather far-fetched. I cannot imagine any man going way back without plenty of ammunition and I simply *can't* imagine a man deserting his partner. For one thing, they are usually too badly scared by loneliness.

'The third yarn is real good. The writer must have had some, otherwise he would not know the habits of dogs, water holes and trails...'

(Then follows a description of the habits of dogs and the use of a balancing pole, etc.)

'But there, all this will hardly interest you, even if it is readable.' (As a matter of fact I was deeply interested.)

'I am so sorry this is such a flat kind of

206

letter, so different from what I would like it to be. Just before the stretcher-bearers came for me I wrote in your album. I don't know whether you knew I had done so or whether you saw it, but I wrote "There's gladness in remembrance." It is a very hackneyed phrase but, sister, I do mean it.'

'Thanking you for your great kindness which I will never forget – Oh I guess I'll ring off. I can't write letters for peanuts. Goodbye.

'Yours very sincerely,

'——'

The following extract from a Public School boy's letter gives a typically twentieth century account of the field of glory and honour, and of our noble warriors' way of regarding things.

'Had a short strafe yesterday and chucked quite a bit of stuff at the Boche, hope it wiped out some of the swine. I love bang, bang, banging away and am looking forward to a great shove one day. Sorry I missed the Somme, even though it was – well, what it was.

'The Boche dropped stuff pretty near my part one day and, discretion being the better part of valour, I did a temporary evacuation. They also at various times have snipped three bits out of my tunic, – dirty dogs, when they know I'm so far from Saville Row!!

'We came out last night and did about thirteen miles back from the line. We're now in a nice, quiet bit of country where we don't expect a 5.9 through the billet, or to awake in the middle of the night at the sound of the gas gong to fix helmets.

'We are quartered at a farm where I've already inspected all live stock and made love to a ripping old thing in the doggy line. The hairies are in the open. They are the worst off as usual and they need all the attention we can give them to carry us through.

'By the way, they're letting me put up a pip, so that spells L-E-A-V-E.'

April, 1916.

'DEAR LITTLE MOTHER – I suppose you got my letter written in Southampton Water and haven't had time to answer it. I hung on to P—— all the way across, good chap, but proper old country boy when travelling. We had a beautiful journey across the ditch and thoroughly enjoyed our breakfast even though it consisted of Easter eggs, dyed purple.

'We had a very nice train journey here and then discovered we were going to a brand new hospital at which we were the first patients. There were crowds waiting at the station with lovely cars, and the cheering and handwagging was something awful. However they finally got us to hospital without running over too many kind people.

'We have a very good time here, motor drives, cinemas, concerts, etc. *but* three times this week I have been to a dentist. On Monday he pulled, pushed and otherwise induced seven of my teeth out. On Friday he put in a mine, I think, and blew out some more. Then he dynamited again yesterday so my mouth feels like a crater. Oh I *am* enjoying life.

'I am jolly glad the gramophone repairs are still holding out. I hope you are going strong, Little Mother, and have nice boys in the ward and that they are taking care of you.' (The *boys* taking care of *me*, forsooth!)

'I think I'll shove in the clutch and foot brake now and switch off.

> 'My very kindest regards,
> 'Yours very sincerely
> '____'

'DEAR LITTLE MOTHER – Just a few lines from the East to tell you I am in harness once more, in a different part of the world this time. I sent you a card but doubt very much if you get it, being a picture card, and they seem to be taboo. My address is...and I should be very pleased and grateful if you would write. I mustn't tell you where we are now. You *might tell the enemy!!!!*

'Coming out I chummed with a boy

from your town. He is very comic and we are such close chums that people call us Pontius and Pilate. Not very nice names, are they? I'm sure you would have found us better ones.

'Well, Little Mother, I don't want to bore you too much so with my very best wishes,

'I remain,

'_____'

Chapter XXIV
Ugh!

February, 1917.

BEING IN THE middle of my second year in France I thought I had sampled active service under every climatic condition, but this past fortnight has introduced me to a new phase, – active service during a black, hard frost, thirty and even more degrees of it.

We awake to find our camp wash-basin sheeted with ice, our whilom hot water bottle crackling with ice, our toothbrush a solid mass, our sponge hard, our tooth paste frozen in its tube, our boots stiff as boards, our chilblains insistent and persistent, – especially those on the heels, – and our bootlaces flagellant to those on the fingers.

A WINDY NIGHT – BUT THE PRECIOUS THERMOMETERS ARE SAVED

In the wards (tents, of course) everything that will freeze has frozen. The thermometers, customarily standing in a small jar of carbolic solution, are found embedded in a little, icy mass. This thawed, and a few temperatures taken, one tries to chart the same. Then the fountain pen refuses to fount. The ward ink? Frozen, also.

One begins to get ready the dressing trays and lotions. Most of the lotions are frozen. Hence, round the ward fire in the early morning is a somewhat crowded collection. First and foremost all the fire buckets, then numerous big and little lotion bottles, their corks removed, and a piece of gauze over the mouth of the bottle. Then sundry medicine bottles.

Giving the medicines in a 'line' consisting, say, of eight marquees is quite a lengthy business. The medicines are primarily all to thaw. Some indeed, the ferri. and amm. cit. for example, are a solid mass, and on more than one occasion the mass has broken the bottle.

Castor oil one finds to be a kind of emulsion, which must also go through a thawing (a slow one, unfortunately), process. The medicine towel is frozen, and one must melt some ice to obtain a little water to wash the glasses.

On trying to make an egg-flip, the eggs are discovered to be frozen, and on going to procure a drink of milk and soda, the milk is found to be solid, and a debris of broken glass, and a straggling little sheet of ice give testimony to what has happened to the soda water bottles.

Then a message comes that the water supply has failed owing to the frost, and that only half a pailful of water per dual marquee is available until the water carts come in three hours' time.

'The water for dressings only,' one reminds the men. That means none for shaving, for washing patients – 'Faith! It's too cold to wash,' says Pat, in true boyish relief – for washing breakfast dishes, for scrubbing, – though truth to tell, the water has sometimes frozen on one end of the table while the other end was being scrubbed, – or any for hot water bottles.

Fortunately, all the hot water bottles are filled with water either in cold liquid, or more frequently in solid form, and they are hung round the stove for the contents to melt before being re-heated.

This morning I encountered one bag which had been knocked out of bed, and the contents were as hard as a brick. The bed patients we keep deliciously warm with lots of blankets, large bed-socks (as many pairs as desired) and woollen clothes from head to heel, 'cholera belts,' nightingales, gloves, balaclavas, anything warm and woolly they care to have.

The up-patients congregate round the stoves, and with the tents laced up and blankets hung over the openings, it is quite an easy matter to keep cosy.

We occasionally laugh at the men dressed *cap-à-pie* in bed, but we nursing sisters are only a degree or two less thorough. Indeed, preparation for bed is a great event.

We all set going our various types of oil-stoves and Tommy's cookers with water for hot bottles, washing and hot drinks. The bunk is a regular Moab, for we do all our 'big washes' at night lacking the courage to do so in the morning. Some mornings we had no wash-water brought us at all, for our supply had frozen, and the choice rested between using that out of our hot water bottles, or waiving the edict of the powers that be forbidding the use of powder, and just indulging in the advice of beauty-specialists, and giving oneself a good 'dry-clean.'

The 'big wash' over, one brews the hot drink – tea,

café noir, café au lait or chocolat, or, perhaps, a glass of vin rouge made hot, and served with a little sugar and a slice of lemon, vin rouge at un-franc-dix the three gill bottle and forty centimes back on the return of the bottle!

Then one caresses and anoints one's chilblains on toes, heels, fingers, and ears, rubs glycerine and red lotion into one's cracked chaps, face cream on one's frost-bitten face, and glycerine on one's cracking lips, dons pyjamas, nightdress, bed jacket, bed socks, bed stockings, piles on the bed dressing-gown, travelling rug, and fur coat, tries to read in bed, and finds it too cold to have one's hands from under the bedclothes, thinks of the home folks, to whom one ought to have written, and of the five minutes sewing one ought to have done, decides it is much too cold for any of them, turns out the light, and cuddles down, hoping that one may go to sleep and remain asleep until 'reveille' without the necessity of having to sit up in bed and massage numb feet or knees, or without having to get up to do physical exercise of the On-your-toes-rise-lower-rise-lower variety.

Besides, one must remember, this is the better weather for the men in the trenches, and so long as we have this hard, dry cold, we don't have those poor, dreadful, blue, purple-black, swollen trench feet among our cases.

Chapter XXV

O.A.S. Hospitality

IT SOUNDS SOMEWHAT Irish in the saying, but it is none the less true that the best part of the day is the night.

After mess dinner at eight, the day nursing staff is free until 7.30 next morning, so it is then that we do our 'entertaining.' This consists of going to one another's bunks or bell tents, and having coffee and biscuits and fruit and chocolate – and conversation.

The hostess usually receives us in bed, which is wisdom on her part, for she is out of the way, and that is an important factor in an area where even inches count. The 'guests' are customarily in dressing-gowns, garments which are as varied as the costumes at a fancy dress ball, and which hail from the sphere of our fighting grounds. There are dressing robes bought in Valetta, burnouses picked up in bazaars at 'Alex,' checked *matinées* from *les galleries* in the nearest provincial French town, little turned up slippers from Salonica, boudoir mules bought in Paris and jeered at because they are not of O.A.S. stability, comfortable stodgy English slippers knitted by comfortable stodgy English aunts, and utilitarian 'slip-ons' hailing from Oxford Street.

'O.A.S.' is responsible for some dreadful lapses and some fearful makeshifts. Our meals and our crockery are most unconventional. To-night we drank black coffee from the cup-screw of a vacuum flask, the cup-casing of a spirit flask, a medicine glass, a marmalade jar, a 'real china' cup, and a piece of porcelain which in peace days was used to contain face powder, and which was accepted with the remark 'To what base uses...' We hadn't a spoon, only a silver button hook. We ate biscuits from the tin. We ate sugared strawberries, – delicious little wild ones, – with a pair of scissors.

We talk as gourmets of the food we eat, and discuss the 'cakes from home,' dilating on the excellence of the cook, whether she be fat, autocratic, and of long domestic standing, or whether she be a young sister just rawly recruited from a domestic science school. Our tastes, too, are catholic.

We partook heartily one night of lobster, cheese biscuits, black coffee, 'plum cake' from the canteen, and slept just as heartily, and next day laughed equally heartily at the rueful dismay of an old dug-out of our acquaintance, who envied our digestion and rosy cheeks.

Of course, like all nursing and medical people we 'talk shop.' One asks the sister from the recovery hut how the boy is progressing she sent for operation, and one of the theatre sisters answers X's inquiry about her trephine case, and Y's question about her amputation case, and we grow keenly interested in descriptions of others, until the girl who sleeps next to the theatre-sister with only a partition between them vows she trembles with fear at the possibility of the said sister coming over in her sleep with a penknife as scalpel and curling tongs as artery forceps.

The smile she raises is well timed, for the conversation has taken on a tragic tone. The sister from the recovery hut has told how one patient on the dangerously-ill list did not want her to write to his wife 'because there is a new baby coming this week,' of how word has come through from home that 'little

221

'sonny's' mother is dead, and he must not be told yet, and of how another boy – only nineteen – had opened dying eyes to see some flowers she had taken into the ward, and how pleased he had been for it reminded him of the garden at home. We sit on the floor of the bell tent and gaze out into the night, a night when the sound of the guns is insistent. Our eyes seek the horizon, and we suddenly feel a helpless band of futile women, agonisingly impotent.

'Well, I must go, and thanks for your cold coffee,' the theatre-sister remarks. Her little piece of *naïveté* dispels our feeling of sadness. One's moods occur in patches on active service.

Only one night in several months have we had an enemy aircraft alarm. We had brushed our hair convivially, and the early birds had retired to rest when we heard the 'Stand to' bugle sounded, followed by 'Lights out' and 'Fall in at the double.' Racing cars, and the sound of many marching feet were the next sounds, and then came a message that each nursing sister had to go to her post, for ours is a tent hospital, and a marquee burns in three minutes, – which is not a great deal of time in which to remove helpless patients.

The first remark would have delighted the cynic. 'What shall we wear?' called one girl from the darkness, the seeming frivolity of the question being set aside when she wondered if, from force of habit, she should go in ward uniform with its preponderance of white, or in dark coat and hat. The next remark got a laugh, and cries of 'Good old Scotty,' for it was 'I'm going to take my money, in case the hut gets hit.'

In a very few minutes we, our identity and burial discs accompanying, were at the doors of the wards, not entering in case of waking the patients, but gazing expectantly up into the sky, and trying to feel as thrilled and frightened as we ought to have been.

But the aircraft was beaten back, and all we suffered was the loss of an hour's sleep, and a little unnecessary preparation on the following nights of placing in readiness gum boots and thick coats.

Chapter XXVI

Night Nursing with the B.E.F.

I DREADED THE very thought of night duty with its tense anxieties, its straining vigilance, its many sorrows. Still I had come to France to 'do my bit,' and that bit for two months meant night work. On active service, too, one quickly becomes inured to doing many things one dislikes and detests; any one with the slightest particle of unselfishness could not fail to become otherwise.

'Half-past six, sister'; the batman clumps along the corridor of the hut in stalwart army boots, making enough noise to wake the Seven Sleepers, and night nurses are far from being in the same category as those enviable beings. Half-past six, dinner at quarter-past seven, twenty-five minutes in which to lie persuading one's self to get up before the reluctant dive from bed

NIGHT DUTY, 2 A.M.

must be made. It is at first strange to go on awaking to a meal of roast beef and boiled turnips, etc., in place of the bacon and eggs to which we have for years been accustomed. Still we are adaptable people, and one must eat to live as strenuously as we do.

We each take our lighted lantern as we leave the mess, and trudge down to the many rows of long tents whitely glistening under the streaming light of a brilliant moon. A dear old major of the old school meets us and bids us 'good-night,' addressing us as 'My Lady of the Lamp.' One of the band, however, very much of the new school, thinks 'the Hurricane Girls' would be a better title for us, and suggests we could become a passable item in a modern revue – song and chorus, the final effect being to black out the stage for a 'lamp dance.'

The weather is a very important factor during night duty in a camp hospital. Each nurse has four to – well, 'x' – number of tents allotted to her, the number depending on her status and on the division, the medical division having a larger number to each nurse than the heavier surgical division. The nurse passes from tent to tent very many times during the night, her work alternating severally from indoor to outdoor, while the distance she covers is quite surprising. One, gifted with a healthy curiosity, attached a pedometer and found she had walked a little over sixteen miles in the night.

Pathways have been made and planks laid down between each marquee, but French mud would defy Macadam's very ghost. We have had nights when wind and rain have raged and lashed, when our hurricanes have blown out directly we have lifted the tent flaps to go out, when we have been splashed to the knees with mud, when even our elastic-strapped sou'westers have blown off, when the rain has stung our cheeks like whipcord until finally with the desperation, the resource, the delightful disregard for personal appearance common to O.A.S. conditions, and owing to the urgency of our need, we have made of our skirts a pair of trousers by pinning down the middle, have stuffed the end of these 'garments' into the tops of our gum boots, tied on our sou'westers with a bandage, and then – got along much more quickly, of course.

The resource and ingenuity of one sister who nursed infectious cases in a camp of small marquees situated in what had once been an orchard, and who to meet the exigencies of her somewhat amphibious work, had a wet-and-wintry-weather skirt made from a ground-sheet, could not be adequately acclaimed.

The rain is occasionally responsible for some few strenuous minutes. Thus the other night a sudden gust of wind accompanied by driving rain burst open the dual outside doors of a hut, the dual inside doors leading to the theatre, and also several windows.

I ran to close the doors snatching up on my way two green-lined umbrellas which figure in sun-cure cases. These I gave to men with limbs on extensions, and whose beds could not be moved immediately. Much amused they were to lie in bed with an open umbrella at two o'clock in the morning. Beds were drawn out to escape open windows or a leaking roof, mackintosh sheets placed on beds that could not be drawn aside until the orderly could be summoned, bowls placed to catch the drippings from the roof, then help was obtained and the two cases of beds plus extension apparatus had to be dealt with.

Night duty during winter weather is somewhat of a Dantesque affair alternating between an inferno of cold and work-filled, perhaps grief-laden, patches of light. The marquees are very cosy, tightly-laced blankets wherever doors occur, and stoves cheerily filled. Between each marquee one dodges up to the knees in snow and slush buffeted by wind and sleet, and dipping under the eaves of the snow-laden tents with ill-luck as dogged as in tilting the bucket. In the surgical tents, – where dressings have sometimes to be done every four, and sometimes every two hours, – one develops into a quick-change artiste at shedding and donning garments.

The normal outfit of a night nurse on winter duty consists of woollen garments piled on cocoon-like under her dress, a jersey over the dress and under the apron or overall, another jersey above the apron, a greatcoat, two pairs of stockings, service boots or gum boots with a pair of woolly soles, a sou'wester, mittens or gloves (perhaps both) and a scarf.

But there are other nights, nights of spring and early autumn with sheets of streaming, silver moonlight when not a breath stirs. The tent walls are rolled back, and looking down the alley of marquees one can see way down to the silent valley below, nights of radiant, faultless beauty bringing to mind Omar Khayyam's stanza, and Matthew Arnold's 'Apollo Musagetes,' nights at one with peace and meditation or with nightingales and love, but with foul carnage and blood lust, man's enmity and man's agony – No!

Once on a time I held the extraordinary opinion that night nursing was dull, that all the nurse did was to arrange the patients' pillows, give a few sleeping draughts, hot drinks, hot water bottles, an occasional dose of cough mixture, put out a light or two, shade others, and sit down to do a little sewing to prevent her being bored before morning came, and the patients were to be washed, and beds made.

That, by the way, was in the days before the war, when I had no acquaintance with ghastly wounds which require dressing every two hours, when the multiple-wound case was the exception and not the rule, when a ward which was then considered acute we should now regard as full of 'convalescents,' when cerebral hernia, tracheotomy, trephine, colotomy, laparotomy, and the evil-smelling gas gangrene were comparative rarities, and certainly not to be found in any one batch of patients, when convoys were unknown, and there was no possibility of the tent-door being pushed aside in the middle of the night, and new patients in the form of pain-wearied men in dirty khaki being deposited on one's beds.

My introduction to active service night nursing was a small hut under the same roof as the theatre, a few of the more anxious cases being brought there for special watching.

Poor boys, almost every patient in addition to other wounds and injuries, had had a leg amputated, and I used to go round from one to another in the dimly-lighted ward with an electric torch, and flash on the light to see that each stump was correct and there was no sign of haemorrhage.

With regard to work on 'the lines,' so far from being dull, one is kept ceaselessly busy, for, in addition to dressings, many four-hourly foments, four-hourly charts, periodical stimulants and feeds, – the latter including jaw-cases where the mouth must be syringed and washed and the india-rubber tube attached to the feeding-cup cleaned and boiled, – there comes the unending, infinitely pathetic call of 'Sister, sister, may I have...' a drink, my pillows moved, my heel rubbed, now my toe, my splint moved, my bandage tightened, my bandage slackened, the tent or the window closed – or opened – a blanket off, a blanket on, a hot-water bag, a drink of water, of lemonade, of hot milk, of hot tea, now a cold drink, sister, to cool my mouth, a crease taken out of the under-sheet, the air-pillow altered, my hands and face washed, my lips rubbed with ointment, my fan, that fly killed, a match, a cig-arette lighted, another drink, some grapes, my apple peeled, a cushion under my arm, under my back, a pad of cottonwool under my heel, knee, arm, a bed sock put on, the bed-clothes tucked in, I feel sick, I can't go to sleep. Shall I have an antiseptic, – the almost invariable name for anaesthetic, – 'to-morrow when my wound is dressed?' Then when the gamut is exhausted – 'What time is it?' 'What kind of weather is it?' 'Can't I have a prick, sister? Can't I have a comforter?' (hypodermic injection). 'Ask the M.O. when he comes.'

There are times too, when one hurriedly tiptoes along the ward at the mention of 'sister' only to find that it is not a call for help, but merely a patient talking in his sleep.

Oh, the glad pleasure and the relieved happiness occasioned by a goodly orchestra of many-sounding, many-toned snores! Then one feels that one's 'boys' are at last in comfort and at ease. No wonder so many poets have chosen sleep as their theme, for an inestimably precious gift it is to the over-wrought, pain-wracked body. Cases of insomnia are fairly infrequent with us, for the boys are usually 'dog-tired' by trench life, which, with its myriad dangers, has developed among our men the restless, broken, fitful sleep of the hunted animal. So our boys either sleep exhaustedly, the sleep of complete physical weariness, or they sleep brokenly. Thus the R.F.C. boy flies busily each night, invariably in trouble about gauge or propeller or because 'she is sulky and kicks.' The Canadian admonishes a rebuke presumably to another Canadian. 'Don't swear so much, mate. There'll be a curse brought down on the place if you swear so much.' Meanwhile the Corporal is 'getting the wind up,' in dire distress because the rations are not getting through.

'Sister, I've lost my letter and two bottles of stout,' calls out a delirious patient. 'We'll find them to-morrow when it is light.' 'Sister, where is my shrapnel helmet? That man washed himself in it, and never gave me it back.' 'I got it from him, and it's in your locker now.' 'Sister, aren't the stretcher bearers coming? Aren't they ever coming? Oh, look, sister, somebody's going to get hold of me. They're nearly up to me. I can't stand up for my leg. Somebody's tied my feet. Where's my rifle? He's got me, he's got me, and I haven't my rifle...Oh God!...Oh, my leg. Oh, for a taste of good sweet water. Mate, your hands are free, and I can't bear this. Shoot me, mate, shoot me.'

'Died in hospital.' 'What a pity,' say some people, 'that he was brought the journey just to die.' But it was not a pity at all. Friends of men who have died in hospital have the great consolation of knowing that they had a comfortable bed, drinks for which they crave, at will. They were warm and well tended, and they had – most blessed of all! – drugs. Thank God there is opium and omnopon and morphia to still such delirium as the above.

Naturally, we have had nights never-to-be-forgotten, nights of aching anxiety and grim, gruesome tragedy, nights that have seared themselves into our brain for as long a time as we shall possess human knowledge and human understanding, nights when we have shared and suffered with delirious patients the stench, the choking thirst, the sound of groans, – all the devilish horror and wracking torture of living again the eternal age with its waiting, waiting, waiting in No Man's Land, nights when a dying man on whom morphia has had no effect has persistently cackled ragtime while another, – one of the very, very few who have realised they are in the Valley of the Shadow, – reiterated again and again 'I'm dying, I'm dying, I'm dying.'

There are moments, too, that have seemed a life's span, tense moments when we have fought for a life with strychnine, morphia, salines, nutrients, and hot-water bottles, crowded moments when, our lamps throwing Rembrandt shadows and gleams round the dark tent with its rows of huddled, maimed forms, there has been plugged and stemmed a haemorrhage from a place where the surgeon could not ligature,

A NIGHT BIRD

reverential moments when one has stood wiping the dew from the face, taking the clutching hand that perpetually seeks to hold to something, moistening the lips of him who is passing through the Valley of the Shadow. One's eyes smart and feel filled with salt as a man with life ebbing, – oh! so painfully quickly, – grasps one's hand and says 'Sister, God bless you.' The full meaning of the remark arrests one, its sanctity, its solemnity, the benedictory significance of the words spoken under such circumstances engulf one. It is not as the smug person would say – one feels amply rewarded for what one has done. Not at all. One only feels so utterly unworthy and mean and small.

But the longest night ends and joy cometh with the morning. The restless tossings have ceased, the breathing is soft and regular. The dew-laden air accentuates the foetid smell of the wounds. I go to the door of the marquee to roll back the walls, and I lean for a moment against the bamboo pole, a surge of emotions overpowering me – aching pity, immeasurable sadness, a sense of human limitations – often indeed – human impotence. Then the joy of success, the transcendent happiness of helping to snatch back a life from the Gates of Death.

And there afar and unwavering, a pale primrose

star, the inky darkness giving way to a soft grey-blue silver-lined, then a pink flush heralding a thousand shafts of ruddy, glowing light, and – rosy as our hopes, radiant with promise – there breaks the Dawn.

Chapter XXVII

Under Canvas

FOLLOWING ON THE coming of the American units to our neighbourhood, we have had quite an influx of nurses, and had to give bed and breakfast accommodation to so many other passing guests, that almost half of our staff are again under canvas. I fortunately am among the tented crowd. I say 'fortunately' for the weather is most friendly – indeed, it is ideal canvas weather. A 'canvas existence' is great fun. It has its pros and its cons, but the pros are so delightful as to outweigh the cons, especially when these latter are made light of with true active service philosophy. The dog walks into the bell-tent in the middle of the night and rudely awakes one by vigorously licking one's face, and exhibiting other unseemly symptoms of canine affection. The bantam proclaims about 3 a.m. that he is roosting on the foot of one's bed, by violently crowing in a piercing falsetto, an unappreciated solo, from which he refuses to desist even though he has hurled at him a damp sponge, a rolled-up knot of a handkerchief, a comb, an orange, and many a 'Shoo, Christopher, shoo, you little wretch!'

Field mice scuttle across the doors on early morning travels as we dress, insects always and perpetually hold high revel, earwigs are discovered holding a confab in the folds of one's apron, while one nurse is found asleep with a lighted candle in her tent – No, she isn't ill, only left on the light to scare the rats.

Yes, it is ideal canvas weather, weather when it is delightful to lie in bed at night and gaze through leafy, high acacias to a far, far, interminably far, blue-black, star-studded sky. It is delightful to pause for a few hours in the rapid whirl of a crowded life, and watch a grey mauve twilight linger over a Corot landscape. It is delightful to lie and watch the soft, gold light of the early sun spangling innumerable diamond dewdrops. It is delightful to hear the rain pattering on tent roof, and to smell the good smell of refreshed green things and damp earth.

It is not quite so delightful, however, to be awakened

in the wee, small hours by the rain pattering on one's face, to be obliged to get up hurriedly, scramble into slippers and raincoat, and go out sleepily and stammeringly into the darkness to fumble and fasten down tent ropes and tent flaps, which latter have been well turned back because the evening was originally so warm.

Then, too, it is not quite so delightful to find the rain invading the tent and again pattering on one's face, especially when two people are sleeping in a bell-tent, and the opportunities of evasion are thus halved. For the geometrical fact rarely finds more graphic demonstration than in this particular application, – half a bell-tent is considerably less than a whole. Still, what would you? A leaky bell-tent is not so bad as a leaky dug-out.

It is somewhat in the nature of a drawback, too, to go on duty on a beautifully fine morning, and to come back after a drenching shower to find one end of the bed sodden, to see a pair of shoes with a little pool of water in the ball of each foot, – it will be days before they dry, – and to make the pleasing discovery that the rain has been joyously cannonading on one's best outdoor uniform. Leaves, spiders and wood bugs in one's wash and bath water are frequent occurrences, while overnight the acacia leaves flutter upon one's face and hair with persistent, babies-in-the-wood effort. Towards creeping things one grows to an amazing tolerance, indeed, to a live-and-let-live nonchalance, a mild interest which would have astounded one in pre-war days. For what is the use of killing a busy, little, shining, black chap of a beetle as he skuds across the tent floor? Nature is so bountiful that she breeds for a higher rate of mortality than we can ever inflict. So even though we squash with the heel of our slipper every spider, earwig, wood-louse, and beetle we saw that would not ensure our immunity from invasion, nor our clothes being free of others when we take them down from the tent-peg.

Instead, we let them get on with that tremendous business called life and give preliminary inspection of our clothes before dressing.

Life in a bell-tent is very circumscribed and circumvented. Though one possess ever so little wealth, wardrobe or worldly goods, still is it difficult to encompass all including camp-bed, camp-bath, basin, chair and a trunk within a floor space whose radius is six feet. And πr^2 minus a tent-peg wholly and completely surrounded by a collection of dressing-gowns, overalls, coats, skirts, mackintoshes and great coats, is a very tight fit. When, moreover, one shares the bell-tent with a second person, one at times comes to the conclusion that the world is too much with us, and it is just a little difficult to love one's neighbour as one's self.

Life under canvas is a very public affair, a very free and easy affair. It is surprising what a barrier is swept aside when one doesn't possess a door. I can only suppose Diogenes had a lid to his tub, otherwise I can't conceive how he managed to philosophise. For life under canvas is very provocative of conviviality.

All and sundry passers-by see one seated within the wigwam and pause for conversation, which invariably gets drawn out, and just as invariably gets extended to impromptu hospitality. The entertaining is alfresco. Usually the guests overflow on to the grass at the door of the tent. A stove burns, merrily boiling water for coffee, two girls sit sewing in deck chairs. One pores industriously and disgustedly over some darning. Two sit on the floor of the tent with arms round their knees, and looking like two little Hindoo idols.

Darkness is falling. A candle in a hanging lantern is lighted within the tent. The warm glow of candle light, the cosy glow of the stove, the grouping, the triangular

'PETTICOAT LANE'

outline of the tent, the background of acacias, the dull grey-blue, silver-streaked sky, – the effect is charming.

The hostess calls across offering a cup of coffee, to be met with the unfailing, active service affirmative.

'Thanks awfully but bring it across, old dear. I'm in bed reading how the war is progressing,' – the only uninterrupted time one gets for the deed.

Numerous good-nights by and bye are exchanged and return invitations are being issued.

'Do come round to see me, I'm No. 3, Petticoat Lane.'

'Come in to coffee to-morrow night. I'm the centre-piece in the Gutter.'

'You haven't been round to my place for ages. I've moved to Piccadilly you know, No. 2.'

'Oh, by the way did you hear about our moving? We two were in a bell-tent under the trees, and some casual mention was made of its being a damp spot, but we heard nothing further.

'Last night we went for a walk into the forest, and on coming back at the end of an hour were electrified to find the only home we possessed had gone, been moved stock, stone, and barrel, and not so much as a piece of paper or a circle of flattened grass to show where it had been.

'However, it was no use being dumbfounded, so

we set off on a tour round the quarters and finally discovered it with furniture and equipment complete. Funny thing when one's home goes wandering.'

Chapter XXVIII
Active Service Kitchens

I couldn't nurse, but I could cook,' several women have said to me when I have been on leave in England. 'Tell me something about the cooking, and what are the kitchens like?'

The kitchen of a hospital housed in a building which has previously been, say, a seminary, or convent, or chateau, is, of course, the kitchen attached to the building, – enlarged, probably, and equipped more or less well.

The kitchen of a camp hospital usually consists of a wooden roof and a square of cement. On the latter are placed the stoves, with tables adjacent, and with a row of boilers near.

Round the stoves and along by the boilers a wooden wall is erected to keep off draughts. Quite probably the rest of the kitchen will be left open, a welcome and necessary condition of affairs in summer, when a few ground sheets will successfully combat any showers. During the winter the kitchen will probably be temporarily boarded in. A little wooden hut will act as larder if no other more permanent building be near. Our mess kitchen is an example of the utilisation of existing buildings. It consists of two, open-fronted, loose boxes formerly used for horses. One acts as larder, while in the other are accommodated a stove, table, and a boiler for hot water.

Any woman used to a 'well-equipped kitchen,' – a term which often includes shining rows of innumerable and unnecessary pots and pans, patent utensils, special storage jars and elaborately made storage boxes, – would be immediately impressed with the austere bareness, and the outstanding sparsity of things in a camp kitchen. But 'active service' is a term to be translated quite literally and to be given the most comprehensive of meanings.

A utensil is an article to be extensively utilised, and if its use does not justify a strenuous existence it is promptly dumped, for its space is more valuable than its presence. Thus the boilers are busy night and day not merely boiling water, but also acting as porridge pots, stock pots, soup pans and pudding pans. The circumscribed kitchen, too, is the scene of much crowded activity, for here thousands of meals are cooked per day, hundreds of men supplied with porridge and tea for breakfast, a certain number of eggs cooked and rashers of bacon fried, several hundreds of pints of soup made for dinner, meat and fresh vegetables prepared and cooked, milk or suet or bread pudding cooked for some hundreds of men, a great quantity of 'milk-rice' boiled for the 'milk-diet' patients, a certain number of minced and boiled chicken diets supplied, a certain number of custard puddings made, probably a number of fish diets prepared, and several pints of beef tea made.

In the afternoon barley water, more cooked fish, cooked eggs, and some hundreds of pints of tea will be supplied, while in the evening a similar quantity of cocoa will be in demand. Meantime, preparations for the next morning's breakfast and dinner will be proceeding apace, while emergency meals for convoy patients, – stews, soups, tea or cocoa, – may be required at very short notice.

The responsibility for securing supplies rests with the quartermaster. His is the task of ensuring the presence of great quantities of tins of milk, tins of jam, chests of tea, boxes of sugar, bags of rice and cereals, thousands of loaves of bread, tins of beef and vegetables, baskets of fresh vegetables, rounds and joints of fresh meat, gallons of fresh milk, stones of fresh fruit, boxes of dried fruits, tins of butter, crates of fresh eggs, and a very host of other things.

The quartermaster is not a popular person in the Army, for it is his business to detect and prevent waste, extravagance, ill-use of articles, and the dumping of the same before their usefulness is exhausted, – the latter a very vexed question on which there are quite frequently two opinions. Particularly is the quartermaster unpopular on issue days and at inventory times, during which latter equipment inspection takes place, and one's bald brooms and brushes are laid out in naked shamefulness, – they are bald in their very earliest youth from stress of life! – one's little secret stores of linen and hardware treasures dragged into the light of day, and hidden recesses ruthlessly invaded and just as ruthlessly plundered.

At most times, however, the quartermaster, like the banker, reminds one of the phrase in the prayer-book. He is an ever-present help in time of trouble. A camp hospital is put up on a piece of bare ground, probably some miles from a town, and the quartermaster's department acts as a dry-goods-grocery-drapery-coal-restaurant-medical stores. Beds, bedding, and bed linen are required, – the Q.M. Knives, forks, table necessities, cooking utensils, – the Q.M. Cradles, baths, instruments, lotions, drugs, – the Q.M. Chairs, lockers, tables, nails, screws, hammers, – the Q.M. Stationery, pens, ink, gum, – the Q.M. – who dispenses the two latter, by the way, in powder form. Just try to lead a Robinson Crusoe existence in a corner of a back garden, and an idea will be gained of where the quartermaster's work begins, though never of where it ends.

'You are interested in kitchens,' said the Colonel of a base depôt in France. 'Come and I'll show you mine.' So we went to two, large, wooden huts.

'I don't know whether it was justifiable pride or positive conceit which underlies this invitation, but I am very pleased to have had it,' I remarked as I looked round, for the kitchens were beautiful, – spotlessly clean, exquisitely tidy and admirably well-ordered, though at the time, some thousands of dinners were being prepared.

The centre of the kitchen was occupied by stoves and some boilers, the asphalted floor round the bottom of the stoves being edged with whitewash, a device which had its effective appearance as well as its utilitarian purpose. Round the walls, – liberally ornamented with cuttings from the illustrated papers of girls and girls' faces, by the way, – were wooden benches scrupulously clean and boasting a few, highly polished, storage jars which had their origin in biscuit tins.

The dinner which was being cooked consisted of a most deliriously smelling stew made from the Army ration of mixed vegetables and meat, supplemented with fresh onions, carrots and suet dumplings. Many roasts of beef were being cooked in the ovens, some boilers were occupied with the cooking of beans, and others with the boiling of rice, which was subsequently to be served with treacle.

The menus for the past week were written on a sheet of paper pinned to the door of the larder. They made interesting reading, and were at least one tribute to the marvellous excellence of British organisation, that target at which so many spitefully-aimed, and stupidly-directed, little pebbles are thrown.

The breakfast each morning had consisted of tea, bread, fried bacon, boiled bacon, or boiled ham, and, on two mornings of the week, potted meat, and on a third, rissoles in addition.

Tea each day had consisted of tea, bread, cheese and butter, or cheese and jam, with Saturday's and Sunday's meal augmented with potted meat. Supper consisted of soup and bread or biscuits, of butter, cheese and biscuits or bread, with tea or cocoa.

The dinner menus for the week were as follows:

Monday.	Roast mutton
	Meat pies
	Cauliflower
	Mixed vegetable ration
	Rice puddings
	Biscuits.
Tuesday.	Boiled mutton
	Roast mutton
	Stew
	Mixed vegetable ration
	Suet pudding
	Biscuits.
Wednesday.	Roast beef
	Boiled mutton
	Mixed vegetable ration

Jam roll
Biscuits.

Thursday.   Roast mutton
Boiled mutton
Cauliflower
Mixed vegetable ration
Rice pudding
Biscuits.

Friday.   Roast mutton
Boiled mutton
Carrots
Mixed vegetable ration
Suet pudding
Rice pudding
Biscuits.

Saturday.   Roast beef
Sea pie
Stew
Carrots
Mixed vegetable ration
Biscuits.

253

Sunday. Boiled beef
Roast mutton
Boiled onions
Mixed vegetable ration
Dumplings
Rice pudding
Biscuits.

Among newcomers in a neighbouring garage one day was another type of kitchen and as it was a bird of passage I went to see it then and there.

It was a motor field kitchen which was being driven to a part of the French line, and was a gift from some Scottish body, whose name escapes my memory, to the Anglo-French Red Cross.

A very handsome and useful present it was, too. The body of the car was built, of course, in the style of a van. Every inch of space was utilised thoroughly effectually, its restricted space and condensed utility being reminiscent of a restaurant car or ship's kitchen.

At the end behind the driver was a cooking stove enclosing two ringed jets supplied with gas made in an attached cylinder. On top of the stove were two large urns fitted with taps, on an adjacent shelf a few dripping tins, frying pans and other cooking utensils.

No attempt, of course, could be made to roast or fry on anything like an extensive scale, boiling and stewing, that most economical form of cooking, being intended for usual adoption. A sink and tap claimed admiration and the spontaneous question regarding the water supply. That, it seemed, came from a tank accommodated on the roof.

Two benches ran along either side of the car lengthwise, a door being at the end, and having a half section to open and with a small 'counter' attached. Overhead and under the benches were excellent, little cupboards, one being on the drawer principle for the reception of towels, and such supply of linen as the kitchen might boast. A window and the usual electric fittings provided light, and, as we looked round in very emphatic feminine appreciation of the elimination of the unnecessary, and the inclusion of everything that was required, still we gazed and still our wonder grew that one small car could carry so much that was commendable.

Chapter XXIX

My Diary Again

MISS ——   RANK Nurse
CORPS V.A.D.   HOSPITAL Z General
has been granted fourteen days' leave from
8/11/16 to 21/11/16.

   N.B. – She should report her arrival in writing
to the Matron-in-Chief, War Office, London,
S.W., immediately on arrival in England, on
attached form.

                    Signed —— ——
H.Q., I.G.C.,   *Colonel, D.D.M.S.,*
   31.10.16   *for D.M.S., L. of C.*

THE ABOVE TYPEWRITTEN message delivered me one bleak autumn morning sends me into a condition bordering on a paroxysm of joy, not that I am pleased to leave my work and the boys, but that, after

almost thirteen very full and busy months' work, I
long, as do most other people, to go home and for
a fortnight be luxuriously spoiled. Here, there are so
many demands on one's pity, one's womanliness, one's
protection, one's self-reliance, that one becomes a little
exhausted and glad to return for a few days to the free
and somewhat careless existence of pre-war days.

In addition to a warrant to travel issued to 'H.M.
Forces Overseas (in Uniform),' I receive also A.F.W.
3337 – this presumably is to be an alphabetical progress of mine – and learn that it is strictly forbidden
to take on leave bombs, shells, shell-cases, trophies
captured from the Enemy, and Uncensored Letters,
that it is my duty to give no information of a military
nature to any one while on leave in England, and that
I am to have the M.L.O. or R.T.O. vouch for any delay
of journey.

I pack in incredibly short time, join two other
V.A.D.s, and we set off. We interview the R.T.O.,
and receive an *ordre de transport pour l'expédition
d'Armée Anglais,* a very imposing affair of impressive hue and corresponding size. Among the *Effectif,
Matériel et Approvisionnements* is a class that interests us, being the *Nature du transport.* Here we find
that, under the heading of *officiers, sous-officiers, et*

soldats, there isn't room to write *trois infirmières,* so we are classified on the next line with the *chevaux et mulets.*

This is by way of being as good as a Canadian's story of the company commander who wanted some goods transported, and who gave directions that if mules were not available, the matter had to be placed in the hands of a party of intelligent N.C.O.s.

The train by and by meanders into the station, and we climb from the depths of the railway line to the heights of a compartment. Some English officers help us to settle our luggage. We thank them and chatter idly among ourselves. One of the officers asks us how we would like the window, – closed or open. We tell him, and return to our conversation. Another asks us if we object to smoking. We state our wishes, and resume our conversation. Another asks us if the heating of the compartment is rather excessive. We reply, and then retire to our own conversation. Finally, after a time one of the officers blurts out:

'Do talk to us, won't you? We haven't spoken to an English girl for months.'

So we all laugh, and the conversation becomes general until we reach the port of embarkation, when we bid good-bye to our khaki companions, – ships that pass in the night.

On board we seek dinner or its nearest approximation, and to the usual query of 'What have you?' we receive the reply, 'Pressed beef' – and we have had bully five days out of the past seven! – 'cold roast beef, ham, and tongue.' For a second course we ask for 'something sweet,' and are brought the only article available, jam! plum and apple!!

After our meal we go to our cabins, where the other V.A.D.s and I are so impressed and intimidated by Hunnish frightfulness, and the exceeding power and omnipresence of Hunnish submarines, that we undress, go to bed and sleep soundly until, about 3.30 a.m., the overhead voice says:

'We're not moving.'

'No,' the other inmate of the cabin drowsily agrees.

'Look out and see what is the matter,' coaxes the upper voice.

'Look out yourself,' impolitely suggests the drowsy voice.

'But I can't get out so easily as you,' remonstrates the upper voice.

'Oh, it's all right. Otherwise we would have been torpedoed by now. Go to sleep.'

And we sleep steadily until the stewardess awakes

us. We breakfast, have our warrants examined, jolt happily down the gangway, and into the waiting train. Then on, past copse and hedgerow, by hill and hollow, through little valleys which are a riot, a superb glory of reds and russets, gold and brown. Here is the black-green of fir and pine, the honey gold and bronze of bracken, the sapgreen of turnip patch, the rich deep brown of overturned earth, the chrome yellow of gorse, then a ribbon of water edged by feathery, silver-stemmed birches, and, yes, really – a golf course. How topping to be home again!

We positively have battalions of rats out here. Awfully impertinent and daring they are, too, – drink out of the fire-buckets in the daytime, sniff round the bread-bin, and generally comport themselves in defiant manner. Last night I was massaging a patient when a rat scurried over my toes. Another night I went to the food cupboard after dark. It is an alcove in the marquee, and I felt something more velvety than the canvas wall brush my hand. It was a retreating rat!

Extraordinary how intense is the interest men can whip up over a rat hunt. The medical ward master occasionally brings his ferrets and puts them under the tent floors. Then sundry fox-terriers and any other available mongrels stand round backed by patients in all stages of convalescence, orderlies, sisters, and M.O.s, biggest babies of all. There is much yapping and excitement, much handling and gripping of brooms and sticks, tent mallets and garden scissors. Yells of execration go up when the rats run out, squealing, to meet their fate. And nothing short of the cookhouse bugle brings the game to a close.

Got a lift by motor-ambulance from town to-day; we were a mixed bag. Sitting beside the driver were two sisters. A V.A.D. was sitting on the knee of the outer one, and I was sitting on a box beside the clutch, brake, and reverse pedals. In the car was a tremendous Brass-hat, 'very metal polish,' as the boys would say, a corporal, two privates, three baskets of fresh vegetables and two bundles of laundry.

We are all rather sorry for ourselves today. We've been taking inventories – 'sufferance is the badge of all our tribe.' For we have been slow to realise that a dustbin is classified as a Bin Ash movable, a folding hospital arm-chair comes under the heading of Chairs Arm HP Fdg, a mirror under Glasses Looking HP, a string doormat under Mats Door Coir, and an enamelled

NOCTURNAL INTRUDERS

dinner-plate under Plates Dinner End...A primrose by the river's brim might have been a simple primrose to Peter Bell, but if that famous rustic had been in the Army he would have needed to be more explicit. Thus, a finger-nail brush he would have had to describe as a Brush Ward Nail. Precept, too, teaches us to call a spade a spade, but the Army requires us to name a hearth shovel as a Shovel Fire Hand.

No, it isn't red tape. It is one of the first essentials in an Army, precision. It is an excellent and very necessary precaution against vague and slovenly wording, which would inevitably incur loss, the duplicating of articles, and much preventable wastage of time and money.

Just now among the patients we have a Russian, a member of the Canadian Army. His name abounds in z, s, k, and y, and other sneezy combinations of letters, but, as he pronounces it, it has a slight resemblance to 'Charlie,' so Charlie he is called.

His language is a most amusing jumble of English, French, and American – all broken, broken sometimes to veriest bits.

He is evidently a great fighter, has been through the Russo-Japanese campaign, and has the clasp of St.

George, first, second and third class, besides other decorations. He loves bombs and machine-guns, and lies imitating the kerer-kerer-kerer-kerer-r-r-r-er whenever he hears the sound. The bayonet, too, he adores.

'Fritzy alway "Merci, kamerad." Yuh, me alway Fritzy stick. Nahpoo, goot-bye, finee Fritzy.'

'Forty-fours' is 'Charlie's' designation of drill, otherwise 'Form Fours.'

'Forty-fours awlri' peace time. No fa' warr. Mills bomb, Lewis, kerrupp, kerrupp, kerrerer, pop-pop-pop war time. Me no prisoner take. Yuh! me Fritzy stick. Uggh, ouch!' and he rolls his eyes and puts out his tongue in just a little too realistic a manner.

One hand-to-hand encounter with a Boche he so described:

'Me Fritzy throat try catch. Fritzy of me the fingers eat' – the Boche had bitten him. 'Me Fritzy jaw with both hands pull. Fritzy ouch, uck! Jawbrok.' Then as a little French *blanchisseuse* trips along the highway with a bundle of laundry:

'Soam swell chicken, that.'

'Me sick, ma warch sick,' he assured us one day when his watch had lost time.

'Me nar goot. Sick soldier nar goot. For soldier want husky guy. Me much sick. Me swing leat, nar.

264

Two blarnkets, wootten cross, finee,' though his despondency was not deep enough to prevent him from admonishing a youth, – with whose opinion on some matter he did not agree, – in choicest Russo-Americanese:

'Hang crep on yar noase. Yar brain's deat.'

The night staff, who, of course, sleep during the day, have given the day people a hint of quietude by posting on their hut a little notice on the lines of the famous caution from the French Government:

'Taisez-vous. Méfiez-vous,' it reads. 'Les oreilles dormants vous ecoutent.'

The orderlies had a farewell supper tonight before being disbanded on account of the Americans taking over the hospital.

They came to the officers' mess to serenade, sang 'Auld Lang Syne,' 'He's a jolly good fellow,' and, – and this was very sweet of them, – 'When you come to the end of a perfect day.'

The latter appealed to me, more especially as I heard to-day, rather strangely for the first time, that our hospital has the reputation of being a very happy one, and that it is remarked for the good fellowship and excellent working tone which exists between all its members, sisters, medical officers, orderlies, and outside staff. This, of course, is due to our having the very best and kindest of matrons and colonels, both of whom know how to get done thoroughly efficient work in a thoroughly pleasant manner. And that is a gift vouchsafed only to few. Every one is made to feel that her or his work is of value and importance, and what an admirable spur to pleased and proud effort that thought does make!

Went to coffee to-night at W——'s, and there the conversation drifted to the subject of our sisters and their work. One, a Princess Christian nurse, went through the South African and a Balkan war. Another served in a couple of Balkan wars and has a knowledge of foreign affairs one never thought, could exist outside the Foreign Office. This one, a Canadian with, *mirabile dictu,* scarcely a *soupçon* of an accent, is quite a *littérateur* and has a remarkable genius for organisation. That one went through a Balkan war and was a prisoner in the hands of the Bulgars for three months. Another is a New Zealander, who was led to take up nursing through seeing a sister die on their lonely ranch.

Then there was mentioned 'Little Sister,' one of the sweetest, most charming women I ever met, who had been in I-don't-know-how-many countries, and who, of all her experiences, liked best the time she spent on a certain hospital ship in the Mediterranean. She used to tell, in particular, of being one Christmas Day up the Adriatic Sea, where at some port they encountered a couple of hundred Serbian refugees, frail women and old men, young children and tender babies.

So the ship was scoured, every trunk and kit-bag searched for chocolate, sweets, Christmas pudding and Christmas cake just lately received from home, mufflers, stockings, coats, caps, anything useful that could be found.

For two tiny new-born babies those Englishwomen had improvised little jackets of cotton-wool covered with gauze, after the style of a pneumonia jacket, and the mothers they had equipped with warm woollens from their own stock of underwear.

Then So-and-so was instanced. Such a grey little life she had led in a dull little provincial town where she had lived and had her training. War broke out. She joined the service, and was sent to work in a marble palace in Egypt – Egypt, the land of sunshine, the land of colour, the land of a thousand antiquities, the vivid land, the baffling mysterious land, the fascinating, bewitching land!

X——, too, had thirsted all her life for adventure, and for thirty years life had been totally humdrum. But when war came she was sent to Salonika, where the sisters had to live in marquees – with hundreds of flies – because bell-tents could not withstand the sandy winds, and where occasionally they had to leave the marquees for the safety of dug-outs because the place was being bombed.

From there she went to a hospital ship, which was torpedoed, she consequently having to spend three hours in the sea. Her next sphere of activity was a C.C.S., which later was bombed. Life in a camp hospital she found somewhat tame, but we assured her she was such a Jonah that something thrilling would no doubt befall us when she had been long enough with us to make the spell work.

Z—— had lived for some months on a barge at a time when this mode of transport was much used for abdominal and spinal cases and fractured femurs. She had been on one of the many hospital ships lined up – a fleet of white and green symmetry – to take the wounded on the evacuation from the Dardanelles. And the evacuation was managed so brilliantly that not a single ship was required. From there she went to a C.C.S. situated in a beautiful French chateau, from there to duty on a hospital train, and then she came to us.

'It is very nice and generous of you,' suddenly spoke a quiet member of the party, 'to give forth such unstinted admiration of our *pukka* sisters, their adaptability and their ability to work under strange and inimical circumstances, but do let us admire ourselves also. The V.A.D.s are not such small potatoes as some people would have them appear.

'Look at G——. She has nursed for ten years, women and children's work, but she has not had general training. Therefore she is a V.A.D., and counted untrained. Q—— is half-way through her M.D. degree, work she left to become a V.A.D.

'R—— is a qualified dispenser and nursed for two and a half years, her training being uncompleted because she had to go with her family to the States. W—— is a fully trained nurse, but too young to join the Q.A.I.M.N.S., so she has become a V.A.D. until she is old enough to be eligible for the former corps.

'S—— is a duly trained and qualified masseuse. E—— has the South African ribbon. She was in South Africa when war broke out, for her father was an

Army doctor. She nursed there in a military hospital until she caught typhoid.

'And apart from nursing, the V.A.D.s are not purely ornamental. W——, whom for months I never imagined capable of playing "The Blue Bells of Scotland" with one finger, electrified me one day by playing to the boys in the Y.M.C.A. hut. Among other things she is an L.R.A.M.

'Then the home-sister was getting grey hairs one day trying to sift out the batmen's off-duty time so as to be strictly fair and just and to please every one, when Y—— laughed and said, "Make an arithmetical progression of it, old dear," and in a minute she had it all accurately arranged. She's a no mean mathematician, it seems.

'M——, too, I noticed in the wards was pretty good with medicines, lotions, improvising apparatus, and generally fixing up things out of very little. Then one day a carefully guarded secret leaks out. She is a London B.Sc, while N—— is a London M.A.

'I've an idea that if we laid bare the skeletons in more of the V.A.D. cupboards we should find quite a good share of brains attached to them.

'And now, children, though not exhausted in subject, I'm tired of blowing our own trumpet, and, since there is nothing more left to eat or drink, I vote we go to bed.'

Had an afternoon of malapropisms. A boy wrote and told his wife he was in hospital with 'nerve-ritis,' while another informed me he had not had his 'two o'clock mometer.' My momentary puzzled expression earned the assurance that he had 'never had the mometer at two o'clock.' So I gave him the thermometer, and all was well.

'Sister in the next hut wants to know if you will send her an armful of omnopon,' was the alarming message brought me a little later.

Not desiring to aid such astounding extravagance – if not slaughter – I gave the messenger an ampule, but so dissatisfied was he at my meagre interpretation of 'armful,' that I explained, and he went off, smiling broadly at himself.

Boarded a tram-car to-day wherein were seated two French girls and a British Colonial soldier, – a Military policeman.

For a time the girls conjectured as to what the 'M.P.' on his arm-brassard might mean but, failing to come to any satisfactory conclusion, one of them finally plucked up courage and ventured:

'Qu'est-ce que c'est, m'sieu?'

'Oh! that. It means "Mam'slle Promenade."' Then, with true colonial enterprise making good his opportunity, he added, 'Will you?'

The M.O. was questioning the patients to-day about their appetite and diet when one boy volunteered the information that he fancied a bottle of Bass and thought one per day would do him a world of good.

'But Bass is jolly scarce out here, boy,' the M.O. reminded him. 'I can't buy myself a bottle at any price, simply can't get it.'

'Then I'll tell you what to do, sir,' came the quick and unabashed retort. 'Put me on two bottles a day and I'll give you one for yourself.'

A general laugh, the M.O. took up the boy's diet sheet and wrote:

'Stout, pints, one.'

Chapter XXX
A Big Push – July 1916

'*B*LISS WAS IT *in that dawn to be alive, but to be young was very heaven.*'

We knew what to expect. For days and nights past we had heard the guns ceaselessly cannonading. So when the batman woke us at six one morning with the message that every one was to go on duty as quickly as possible, we were not surprised.

We washed, dressed, and breakfasted hurriedly. It was a glorious morning with great glowing shafts of streaming sunlight warmly irradiating the camp. The tent walls had as usual been rolled back, thus making of the wards a roof and a floor. We could see therein a great stir and bustle, but what was it caused a sick pain at the heart and hastened our hurrying footsteps?

In every walk there were wounded soldiers, a

273

bus-load of the more slightly wounded cases at one marquee, motor-ambulances with stretcher after stretcher of more seriously injured burdens bringing up the rear, men being carried pick-a-back by orderlies, others being brought on the 'four-handed seat,' others trudging along with the aid of a walking-stick.

Tunics had been torn to free wounded arms, breeches had been ripped for access to injured legs, boots had been discarded in favour of huge carpet slippers or bandages, heads were swathed, jaws tied up, bandages stained with dirt and blood.

Almost every boy was clay-caked, the hair full of yellow clayey dust, the face thinly crusted with it, the moustache partly embedded in it. One Jock I subsequently found with puttees caked to the legs which were covered with set clay as evenly as a plaster-of-Paris limb.

'Good morning, boys,' we called as soon as we were within speaking distance.

And a very volley, a regular cheer came to our white-clad, white-capped party. 'Good morning, sisters.'

'We'll soon have you fixed up.'

'That's all right. We've shifted them, so it's worth it.'

The first batch of patients we treated stands out in any memory. They were fed, bathed, put into clean pyjamas, had their wounds dressed, were each given Blighty tickets and cigarettes, and lay with faces expressive of the personification of blissful contentment.

Presumably, they had reached the acme of Tommy Atkins satisfaction. But no! A gramophone in adjoining lines struck up a song associated with limelight, red noses, checked suits, flat long-soled boots, and knotty walking-sticks. Immediately those boys howled out the chorus. Their cup of joy was full.

On and on we worked, forgetful of time and remembering our own meal only as we became exhausted. Trestle beds with a paliasse, or donkey's breakfast, as the boys call them, had been laid down in the wards. The church tent, the store tent, and the Y.M.C.A. hut had been requisitioned, and some Indian marquees sprang up infinitely more quickly than the proverbial mushroom.

These took the slight cases of which, fortunately, there was a very large proportion. The expansion, also fortunately, was a matter of speed in treatment rather than excess of numbers.

Every one 'mucked in' in that magnificent wholehearted way British people have when they are 'up against' anything. Armchair critics who love to talk about 'red tape' ought to have seen the work being done. Rank and officialdom were forgotten, chiefly by those who held the one and were held responsible for the other. Every one turned with enthusiasm to the task they had in hand. Stately methods of procedure were most emphatically and unceremoniously dropped. In a big push, in battle, there comes a time, I understand, when it is 'every man for himself.' In the aftermath of a big push, in hospital, it is at all time 'every man and woman for "the men."' And that has to have direct interpretation, whereas in more leisurely times a certain section of the staff, the clerical and the stores section, for example, must, of course, work indirectly for the boys.

Whatever our hand found to do on that memorable day and the four following days, we did with all our might. Our colonel and medical major, kept waiting a few minutes in the middle of the night for a convoy they were to receive, put off their coats and helped cut bread and butter for the coming patients.

A dentist, finished his dental work, did nursing-orderly duty far through the night. The *padre* ladled out soup and tea, at which he said he was an expert through long practice in soup kitchens and at Sunday School teas. He ran about unceasingly, too, giving patients drinks, quite a big item in the case of newly wounded men and with the weather very hot.

He also acted as additional barber and went round with safety razor preparing for our further attention, surrounding surfaces of wounds on shin, cheek, jaw, and head.

'My word, sister,' we were repeatedly assured, 'that razor's a treat; it's a champion. And the *padre!*' – mentioning in an impressed undertone the decoration he wore and the rank he held – 'Sister, he's a real toff. The right sort o' sky-pilot, he is. One o' the best.'

Then, in true Tommy Atkins spirit of refusing to be impressed for too long a time, there would come a little chuckle, and, 'Say, sister, eeh, eeh, eeh, should I offer him tuppence?'

Laughter, tears, immense satisfaction and pleasure, immeasurable pain and disappointment were commingled that day. One lived very many times in a torrent of emotion, agonised by a flood of pity, racked by an intensity of sympathy, tortured by an exquisite, mental pain, almost overwhelmed by the passion to help to fight for those lives.

Oneself at such times lives through an acuteness of mental suffering hitherto unparalleled in life, and one strange, curious self is busily concerned with steriliser and instruments, dishes and lotions, hot-water bottles, extra blankets and black coffee. Then later a chance description of one's self travels back as gossip will do.

'She's one of those calm, collected sort of beings who would have made a good surgeon. Doesn't fuss, you know.'

As ithers see us!

Fortunately.

So the day wore on and night came. Without – a night of glorious July summer, with palest saffron, flamingo and purple lights, and one gem-like star, a night of ineffable beauty and peace, and within – a vision of Hell, cruel flesh-agony, hideous writhings, broken moanings, a boy-child sitting up in bed gibbering and pulling off his head bandages, a young Colonial coughing up his last life-blood, a big, so lately strong man with ashen face and blue lips, lying quite still but for a little fluttering breathing.

The boy goes to the theatre to be trephined – he later made an excellent recovery – the night sister takes charge of the Colonial and his neighbour; the medical officer asks me to have a man's name put on the D.I. list. 'No hope.'

'Sonny, I'm giving out field-service post cards,' I tell

him. 'Perhaps you would like me to write yours and save you the trouble. I'm just taking your mother's address from your pay-book.'

Three photographs drop out, a mother and father in 'Sunday-best' clothes, an elder brother, a gunner, and 'Yours, Alice.' The boy rouses himself from his listlessness to tell me she is 'the best girl in the world, a munition worker' – proudly – 'making thirty shillings a week.'

As I write the address, put away his pay-book, and moisten his lips, the faces float before my eyes. Alice would weep, but the mother and father would just look numbly into the fire. For them there would be no outlet in a passion of grief, only an aching, gnawing want to hear the voice, see the well-set-up figure and the laughing face, that dreary want to be endured so long as life lasted. And the gunner would tighten his lips and feed the guns more determinedly.

The electric lights are shaded to facilitate and invite sleep. The dressings are now only minor ones, and we carry round a tray, and dress by the aid of hurricane lamp and flashlight. Finally we come to the last one, and leave the patients to the night staff.

'Any help required?' we ask our neighbours in adjoining lines.

'No, every one seems to have finished.' So we turn towards the quarters.

For a time no one speaks. Then, 'What a wastage of human life!' comes somewhat bitterly; 'a useless waste!'

'Never!' comes another voice passionately, the tone indicating the strain endured during the long, long day.

'How can the gift of those lives be called a "useless waste"? Is it a waste for men to fight, to suffer, and to die for all that they hold dear – their liberty, their ideals, and their loved ones? God made man in His own image, a little lower than the angels. I've realised that fact anew to-day. I've seen that Man can ascend to almost Godlike heights, to realms of sublimity unsuspected.

'To-day's stories of the fighting, told to us red-hot from the lips of the boys who have lived them, those stories and the many little incidents we have all witnessed, have shown us that, while war may be a great wastage, it is also a great purifier. It has brought out valour indescribable, self-sacrifice unforgettable, patience and magnificent endurance untellable. And are these nothing worth?

'I have heard little scraps of conversation to-day; I have seen little acts of self-sacrifice, kindliness and thoughtfulness between the men, that have made me feel reverent. There may be brutality, bestiality, fiendish recklessness, devilish remorselessness, anguishing mutilation and destruction in war, but to-day I have met fortitude, devotion, self-abnegation, that has brought with it an atmosphere of sanctity, of holiness.

'I am too tired to sleep, too tired to do anything but lie and look up at the wooden roof of the hut, too tired to do anything but think, think, think, too tired to shut out of sight and mind the passionate appeal of two dying eyes, and a low faint whisper of "Sister, am I going to die?"

'But, oh, how glad I am to have lived through this day! With the stinging acute pain of all its experiences raw on me, I say it has been a privilege to undergo these sensations. For the pain will pass, since all pain ultimately dies, but what will endure for ever is the memory of the nobility, the grandeur, the approach to divinity we have all seen. It has made better women of us all; it has brought knowledge to our understanding, life to our ideals, light to our soul.'

Chapter XXXI
'Proceed Forthwith'

'THE HOSPITAL HAS been accepted by the Americans, and will be taken over within a fortnight.'

The official news came like a metaphorical 5.9, notwithstanding the fact that we knew the offer had been made. We had not, indeed, attached a great deal of importance to the fact, for the floating of rumours and the discussion of possibilities, many of which latter never even reach the stage of probabilities, are quite the recognised thing in the army.

Having lived happily, and worked still more happily in the one hospital for twenty strenuous and crowded months, we had all grown to love, if not actually 'every stick and stone' of the place, at any rate their equivalent marquees and tent-pegs. So we had deluded ourselves like the Micawbers, with the idea that 'something

A CORNER OF THE NURSING QUARTERS WITH A 'WIGWAM' AND
TWO 'HEN COOPS' IN THE DISTANCE

would turn up' in our favour, that the Americans might not accept our particular hospital, that it was too large for a unit new to active service, that it might be too far from their base – any old reason would do.

Then following on the news came the order to hold ourselves 'in readiness to proceed forthwith.' What did 'forthwith' mean? It might mean two hours, half a day, a day, three days. At present it couldn't be translated as anything more explicit than 'forthwith.'

Meantime the nursing staff was sent about its business of packing, and while the hut resounded with the scuffliings of twelve busy inmates reminiscent of the tossings and pawings of twelve unruly horses in twelve circumscribed loose boxes, one sister told the historic tale of the nurses who had received similar instructions to 'proceed forthwith' to the War Office. No. 1 went immediately in a taxi, No. 2 presented herself in the evening of the same day, No. 3 arrived next morning, while No. 4 came at the end of three days.

It is all very well in song to pack up your troubles in your old kit-bag, but it is the packing of the kit-bag with overflowing kit that is the trouble. One collects a wonderful accumulation of impedimenta – word deliberately chosen – in twenty months, even if one does live in a bell-tent or in a bunk which measures only 6 ft. by 10 ft. Hence vacilating owners stand indecisively over piles of clothing and equipment, keeping articles 'that really might prove useful' – and frequently don't – while discarding others for which 'there is absolutely no room whatever,' only to find that they are the very articles most required a couple of days later. The Belgian scrub-women receive enough discarded garments to set up an old clo' establishment.

'Can any one lend me anything to poke out drawing-pins?' asks a voice, the owner betraying a typically active-service disregard of the nature of the article supplied, or the person who supplies it.

All penknives and scissors seemingly being already engaged, 'Use a safety-pin,' she is advised. And so armed she sets to work to take down her Kirchner girls, her Bairns-father drawings, her khaki portrait gallery, and her family snapshots.

'Lend me a tin-opener or a safety-pin, Baby,' calls another voice.

'In a moment,' 'Baby' replies. 'I've just discovered that all my stockings are holed and I'm deciding to wear two pairs, so that the holes of the one may not coincide with the holes of the other. Like most riders, it takes a little working out.'

'I'm glad it is cooler weather,' remarks the Sensible

Girl, who always gives us good advice. 'We can wear more clothes and so save packing.'

'Packing! I'm fed with it, and yet I'm surrounded still with things,' grumbles one voice.

'Oh, it's the limit!' growls the second.

'I would I were a daisy,' croons the third sadly.

'You'd still be liable to be uprooted,' comes the level tones of the Sensible Girl in well-timed reminder.

Clothing and personal equipment packed, the camp furniture is next induced into the kit-bag. Certain sturdy wenches undertook this onerous task of inducement themselves, but, remembering the treacherous behaviour of beds that fold in concertina fashion, and of camp baths that collapse like a violin stand, I seek out skilled labour in the person of a long-established batman who has helped very many sisters to 'proceed forthwith' to hospital train, hospital ships and casualty clearing-station.

He deals firmly with the furniture and summarily with the kit-bag, so much so that it and the two other bundles regulations allow are soon quite ready.

'Your orders have come through tonight, movement orders to-morrow,' I am told subsequently, a list of other nurses 'proceeding forthwith' being enumerated.

'We're lucky not to be moved *en masse*. Remember

the night sixty-four sisters left No. Q?' We are not likely
to forget it, for the quarters were a second Caledonian
Market of trunks, valises, suit-cases, spare deck-chairs,
spare tables, buckets, washbasins, vases, straw mats,
small rugs, homemade stools, packing-box furniture,
great sausage-like kit-bags strained to bursting point,
inadequate holdalls and self-advertising contents, discarded hats, boots and lingerie overflowing the refuse
bins, a perfect plethora of impedimenta surrounding
the mess, the huts, and lying round under the trees.

'A few parrots in cages would complete the picture,'
remarked one flippant V.A.D.

Early on the morning following the coming of our
orders, the cars drew up at our quarters, and it became
our turn to 'get moving.' Our own kit-bags, stuffed to
the furthest limit with our beloved Lares and Penates,
are dragged out. Our own holdalls demonstrate an
expressive and contradictory title, for they give positive proof of holding much, and they give evident signs
of allowing much to escape. Suit-cases, attaché cases,
wooden boxes, coats, mackintoshes, and lastly ourselves are packed into the various waiting cars.

We have said good-byes, and give a last look round
at our dearly loved hospital, where we have been so
happy, at the grey, sun-glinted marquees wherein we

have spent so many wonderful, life-pulsating months, at our wooden shacks, our Hans and Gretel 'sugar houses,' 'wigwams,' 'hen-coops,' and 'rabbit-hutches' nestling under the trees. The sorry feeling, a bedrock sorry feeling, will not be gainsaid, when:

'You're forgetting your iron rations,' excitedly calls one of the home sisters. 'You will be glad of these about eleven o'clock to-night when you have drowned your grief and are ready to sit up and take nourishment.'

She hands up to us an active-service size biscuit tin tightly packed with sandwiches, another, – also out-size, – filled with bread and butter, together with a bag of hard-boiled eggs. These we ourselves have supple-mented with a supply of fruit, one or two cut cakes, and the contents of sundry thermos flasks.

The foremost driver cranks his car, the rest follow suit. A group of sisters, batmen, and dogs are speeding us on our parting way.

'Good-bye, good luck, and cheerio,' calls some one. We bid more good-byes, and wave others. The car starts. Peter, the camp pet, a 'dog of sorts' – several sorts, including, more especially, a good sort – jumps on the seat beside us and licks frantically our faces which we have just washed. We caress him ere we regretfully bundle him out, and away we go, Peter with flopping ears and lolling tongue racing after us in a cloud of dust.

We are proceeding forthwith.